The Firstborn Son:
A Curse, a Gift, or a Calling;

The Much-Needed
Cardiac Resuscitation Our Society and World Requires.

Ezechiel "Zeke" Bambolo, Jr.

Ron Davis,

It is a pleasure to meet you and more importantly share the passion of fishing with you. Thanks for sharing your equipment with me and the boys of Heritage Christian Academy.

Ezechiel "Zeke" Bambolo, Jr.

Rom 8: 28-29

The book you now have in your hands is a powerful message that needs to be read and spread throughout North America and beyond. It is worthy of your time and necessary financial sacrifice to secure, carefully read, and prayerfully implement selected principles contained within its pages into your family considerations.

As I read Zeke's book I wondered if the picture he paints regarding the responsibilities of a firstborn son in an African culture are really a mini snapshot of many of the roles and responsibilities which would have been considered normal, rather than novel, in the Middle East, the Far East, and in the homes of Moses and Jesus. My suspicion is that these cultures more accurately reflect biblical perspective than the indifference of being a firstborn son in our own country, at least at this time.

We live in a place and time where respect has been replaced by entitlement. Authority and structure are viewed with ridicule and something to be ignored or rejected as antiquated, bigoted traditions stuck in a time warp. The chaos and entropy we now see as regrettably normal in many of our work ethic, morals, homes, schools, employment, downtowns, and neighborhoods is as predictable as it is repugnant.

Zeke's story from a happy boy to a potential forced recruit bent on murder and mayhem, to a college basketball player and high school coach, through the inhumanity of racism, to a loving husband and father, pragmatically speaking, is not just interesting; it is powerfully insightful and inspiring.

It is my pleasure to highly recommend the reading and distribution of this challenging book and the enduring legacy it promotes and promises. Our culture is crashing around us in North America. This book is a lifeline for help.

Zeke, I am proud to count you as my brother, my friend, and a fellow soldier for our Savior, the Lord Jesus Christ.

Blessings to you and this book!

Dr. Karl I. Payne
Pastor
Chaplain
Author of *Spiritual Warfare: Christians, Demonization, and Deliverance*

First published by Dog Ear Publishing
4010 W. 86th Street, Ste H
Indianapolis, IN 46268
www.dogearpublishing.net

dog ear
PUBLISHING

ISBN: 978-145750-369-6

This book is printed on acid-free paper.

Printed in the United States of America

To my family, my wife, Teena, my daughter, Haedyn Grace, and especially my son, Garrison Asher.

Our heavenly Father has done an amazing job of giving us each other in the bonds of amazing love. I cannot imagine accomplishing anything more in the life God gives me without the joy I get from sharing it with you all. Garrison, the motivation for writing this book begins with you indeed. May God guide me to rise to the occasion and overachieve on the task of preparing myself to be your father and your Elijah. (See 2 Kings 2:9.)

CONTENTS

ACKNOWLEDGMENTS

It has long been said that "No man is an island...." The concept of strength-in-community is incredibly powerful and epitomizes those that have been my support in writing this book. There are some individuals that have been directly supportive and very encouraging as I pursued this project. My wife, Teena, has been an incredible support to me especially in allowing me to share some of our lives' most intimate events. I applaud her for carefully reminding me that God expects us to comfort others with the blessings and comfort He has bestowed on us (see 2 Corinthians 1:3-7).

In addition, there are some who spent the time speaking with me supportively and/or reading initial manuscripts as well as providing experience and advice in various respects. I must acknowledge Dr. Karl Payne, Matthew Freisen, Patrick Gamido, Alice Goldberg-Fading, and Hutch.

Finally, there is a group of key men in my life that have stood by me weekly through much of the latter years refusing to let me be an island. It is your accountability that has taught and encouraged me to live much of what I write about. Truly, without authentic and committed relationships like yours, I run the risk of overwhelming challenges. On the contrary, I have found solace and vigor to follow Christ, God's Firstborn Son amongst many brethren.

FOREWORD

Native Son

When anyone reads this book they will instantly begin to understand faith, intrigue, culture, survival, hatred, separation, reunion, parental love, sibling devotion, promotion of family values, and divine intervention. The life of one African family should be the example of how trust in our Savior will never fall short in our desire to hold onto hope.

Dr. Kenneth "Hutch" Hutcherson
Founder and Senior Pastor of Antioch Bible Church
Redmond, WA
Author of *Enough Faith* and *Hope Is Contagious*

INTRODUCTION

I come from a culture outside of the borders of these great United States in which I now reside, yet also from one family (you and I) unified by the precious blood of Jesus Christ. What a powerful statement of attribute to our God. I was greatly fortunate to have an earthly father who taught me and set the tone from my earliest days concerning my responsibility and requirements as his firstborn son. I have a loving family (siblings and mother) who embraced me as such and honored that birthright to the fullest in times of joy and distress. To depict the full spectrum of effectiveness of the birthright, this book brings you along in times of joy such as fishing trips and other fun moments with my siblings and father. Come along with me and see how the desire and fight to honor the birthright in a noble pursuit came close to costing me one of the most disastrous failures of my life, my marriage.

The book also brings you along to stand with me and see the effectiveness of the birthright as I stand under pressure in the face of death, looking down the barrel of an automatic rifle because of the choice to not deviate from my father's teachings. As such, the legacy of my family instituted by my father is securely being ushered to the next generation in the confines of vibrant and healthy homes by his now adult children. Noting the previous declaration, here is a book that refutes untrustworthy critics of masculine leadership and edifies the distinguished roles of fathering and living as a firstborn son.

It really doesn't take much to incite the naysayers seeking to paralyze our society with the offerings of strange and faulty teachings. Here is a sample scenario. A reporter speaks, "Mr. Williams, today is the greatest day of your life. You have just accomplished a feat that will probably not be repeated for another one hundred years to come. How do you feel about that?" In jubilation Mr. Williams begins his response, "Hi, Mom…" Your local feminist jumps at the chance to proclaim, "Ah ha, here is another great evidence and symbol of the end of masculinity…he chose to speak to his mom first rather than his father. Men are truly no longer relevant."

Folks, there are many a happy and healthy homes in this country. Fathers and husbands, especially those who are strong, protective, sacrificial, and God-fearing men in whose hearts the Lord abides, are ecstatic to see their wives, mothers, and sisters get the glory for being powerful women. Their masculinity is by no means threatened by the social, professional, or matriarchal success their wives achieve. Why? The biblical concept of matrimonial essence and roles with regards to equality in the home (discussed later in this book) easily addresses the question. Not every preconceived agenda-bearing book or article that for years now has sought to prematurely foster the so-called *"End of Men"* and the hostile takeover of women speaks the truth of the matter. The scare tactic of the feminist when verbalized is, "If we can get the culture to think this is indeed the case, we've got them right where we want them. The lie becomes reality for them." Well, they are wrong because Truth is on guard (See John 14:6-7).

This is where this book, *The Firstborn Son,* timely steps in. One of the greatest idioms I remember from my childhood says, "Where there is smoke, there is fire." In other words, if there is even a hint or some whisper of the societal speculation that *men are irrelevant,* the likelihood that there is a wee bit of actual evidence is high. However, if that bit of evidence of the problem is not addressed or if it is fed, it will manifest itself into an overwhelming reality. The treachery of that devastating manifestation (the fire mentioned in the idiom) however is the fact that the problem grows and eventually consumes even those who fed its growth. In short, feminist beware, you are feeding a fire that will consume you as well. Therefore, this book is intended to move us as a society to excellence ordained by our Creator and God of order.

What is this problematic manifestation or fire I speak of? It is the Esau Disorder (discussed in detail later in the book) that we as a society have so easily chosen to embrace. It is the throwing away of the "birthright" that each and every component of society and the family (father, mother, siblings, sons, the church, the government, and so on) have so easily embraced. The reality of our conversations anymore with regards to birthright is simply in the context of our worldly geographic citizenships, or maybe birth order.

The problematic manifestation is the fact that we have lost every hint for understanding the extremely strategic role the firstborn son fills in the context of the family unit and its subsequent generational excellence. I am speaking of matters as simple as the conscious and subconscious adoration of older siblings by younger ones which subsequently triggers the trickle down effect on characteristics such as family temperament. Even more costly and sometimes irreversible is the impact on family because fathers have failed, due to their lack of confidence, to impart their legacy (heritage, traditions, and customs) to the firstborn and thereby easily foster much-needed generational perpetuation. We want to raise our boys to be like famous and historically mighty men rather than the great men (you their fathers) they see most every day of their lives. Given that focus, our boys will never see intimately nor in the midst of vulnerability life's greatest lessons. If your son(s) sees you everyday or on a consistent basis they are bound to see those moments when you are challenged and vulnerable. Those are the moments during which life teaches every father his greatest lessons, and life does the same for our sons who keenly watch us battle those challenges.

The epidemic of single parent homes amongst all races, in many cases by choice due to the lie of the feminist movement, seeks to paralyze our society also. Children-specific statistics of the government spells out clearly the damage this epidemic creates. One such damage is the fact that 65 percent of all African-American homes are headed by single parents, and 96 percent of those single-parent African-American homes are fatherless. As such, these single parents, the majority being women, tend to send their sons (and daughters) out into the world as victims of their circumstances. With evidence this book seeks to educate you and realign your thinking that your circumstance truly provides you (mom and child) heroic resilience, in many cases second to none in this world. As a result, this book confidently teaches you to see and produce not victims but rather the true heroes our society awaits and greatly loves to embrace.

I am not a seminary-trained theologian, but I assertively believe the best teaching is done in the intimacy of everyday practical occurrences. First, there is no greater example for all components of society, especially parents and firstborn sons, than to observe God's role of parent in His relationship with Jesus Christ who has the role of Firstborn amongst many brethren or believers. Christ portrayed the great and holy heritage and pedigree as a successful firstborn son for each of us believers, the brethren, to follow; the trickledown effect within the family of God. As younger siblings you and I have the promise and reality of an incredibly fulfilling life for eternity now and forever if we follow the example of the Firstborn Son. Or, we can have a life of disappointment and doom if we choose not to follow Him.

Christ continues to give us the greatest example of teaching through everyday practical occurrences when He said to His disciples, "Follow Me, and I will make you fishers of men" (Matt. 4:19, NASB). He then proceeded to take the twelve disciples with Him everywhere He went. The result? They changed the world. The greatest apostle, Paul, did the same with his disciples but none more than one he called "his son," Timothy. Timothy was confidently left to complete work his missionary father (Paul) began with no doubt he would be an exact replica of his teacher.

> "For this very cause I sent to you Timothy, who is my beloved and trustworthy child in the Lord, who will recall to your minds my methods of proceeding and course of conduct and way of life in Christ, such as I teach everywhere in each of the churches" (1 Cor. 4:17, AMP).

As you read this book, join me in our desire to share the message and reclaim the virtue of the birthright to the firstborn son in our homes, society, and the world. Here are some key and strategic effects we will achieve for our children's generation:

1. Begin to recognize and reconnect with what the birthright (firstborn son) looks like. The results will ultimately be more selfless and sacrificial men, husbands, and fathers, and a lifestyle that will definitely do a lion's share to correct the direction of the culture.
2. Children would more readily adhere to the family custom and legacy we parents intend to leave rather than disown it.
3. Lighten, but not eliminate, the parenting load by instilling the birthright to its rightful importance and place with the firstborn son. Then take some time to enjoy the trickle down effect.
4. Most importantly, we will give Christ His rightful place, and He will truly be embraced by our children. They will easier accept rather than abandon Him because they recognize the attributes of the Firstborn Son amongst many brethren. Christ will truly be recognized as part of the family, your family, and the foundation of the legacy you pass on.

For our society to address the problematic manifestation, the death of manhood, that is so easily propagated by agenda-laden individuals, we need to restore the attractiveness of the birthright, especially to our firstborn sons and legacy bearers. Rather than take a defensive posture against sources and ideals that are clearly destroying morality within our families and culture, we need to go on the offensive and train our boys (children) to be selfless and sacrificial men ready to embrace Godly, authentic, and holistic leadership. Wherever you find yourself, I truly hope and pray that this book is the answer you need for your specific situation.

CHAPTER ONE:

Do You Understand the Nature and Temperament of a Firstborn Son?

It is a warm, muggy, and humid day, and a few hundred people are being rounded up primarily by young teenage boys carrying AK-47s, M-16s, and other automatic rifles. I am a part of the crowd. A very short moment later, the end of my life flashes before my eyes as I stand in a ravine staring into the barrel of an M-16 rifle whose carrier (about my age or slightly older) has just decided to take my life. Our captors claim I am an enemy combatant who is planning a counterattack on them although it is blatantly obvious I have no weapons. My mother and siblings are also in the crowd, and she begins to plead vigorously for the life of her son claiming I am not an enemy soldier but simply a student. The young man with the automatic rifle, if you can't tell by now, is part of a lawless group of bloodthirsty rebels. He turns to my mother and says, "If he is your son and you are so sure he is not a government soldier recruit, step in and die for him." Approximately five minutes of dialogue with my mother goes by during which she has offered to die if he promises not to take my life, but he gives no such guarantee.

The rebel retrains his automatic rifle on me to finish what he started, and the rest of the crowd is heavily distraught. Many in the crowd who know me well, as well as my family, have been crying and helping to plead with my mother. Just as he is about to open fire and execute me, a sudden eruption of loud cries come from the crowd that startles him. He lowers his rifle, stares a bit, and promises that he will watch me closely in the moments and days to come. He promises that he will execute me at the slightest hint of opposition to his and their cause. You would think that is the worst of this living nightmare, but it isn't. The real battle that ensues is the physical and mental fight for life. The battle to resist peer pressures of other rifle bearing teenagers and men who all desire to conscript me forcefully or willfully, some of whom I know really well. It is obvious that the easiest way to stay alive, especially as a young able-bodied athlete is to take an AK-47 and loot, rape, and pillage like the rest of them. I know they want me to. So, why not...?

Allow me to describe a few other real life events to you and see if you can determine what the outcome would be if it were your life. This chapter of the book is strictly intended to give you a snapshot into the life experiences of the writer and his unique qualification and expertise on this firstborn son topic. But most importantly it will set the tone for personal introspective examination, which I absolutely believe will allow you to get the greatest value out of this book. The experiences described will be revisited in relevant chapters later in the book. So don't fret, you will get the rest of the story. Here are a few questions to ponder as you read the descriptions of each of these real life occurrences:

a) Would you still have the qualifications to claim a successful execution of your role as a firstborn son?

b) Would you have maintained a successful execution of your impressionable role as a father, mother, sibling, or mentor of a firstborn son? Or...

c) Would any of these situations force a compromise of your character such as rejection, conceding under pressure, discriminatory treatment, retaliation, or possibly even result in incarceration?

Fight for Life or Endure Abuse

I was born on the West Coast of Africa in a beautiful little country with some of most wonderful Atlantic beaches. I was the first son of hardworking teachers who gave their children an incredible life of safety and good fortune. By standards of the Western Hemisphere we were poor, but by African standards we lived quite comfortably. I had no idea we were poor. The environment was incredibly rich in worldwide cultural diversity. More importantly, I received an astonishing gift of academic and spiritual nurturing wrapped in a package of innocence that any father worldwide would be proud to give his son. At this point in my life (era), I also have in my possession basketball and musical scholarship offers to a couple of United States universities.

The exact day that I received my high school diploma was December 22, 1989. At this point in my life I also had in my possession basketball and musical scholarship offers from a couple of United States universities. I gave a promising speech in front of my proud parents as the salutatorian of my class. This very day a rumor began to circulate like wild fire. It was a rumor that would prove true and begin a prolonged test to every fiber of my upbringing. It began with the breakout of a nasty and treacherous civil war.

On the first day that I came into contact with rebel soldiers, I was picked out of a group of several hundred people and accused of being an enemy combatant. I now faced execution. The whole group of regular and displaced inhabitants were rounded up from dormitories and homes and moved at gunpoint by several rebels toward the gated entrance of the campus. A friend of mine decided to make a short comment to me about the situation as we marched with arms up in the air. I responded but not quickly enough. A rebel soldier saw us communicate and accused us of planning to launch a counterattack, although we had no guns. The true intent of the rebels in this instance was to instill fear in the minds of their captives, us campus inhabitants, by conducting an execution for all to see. That was the best way to ensure no one would dare oppose them. Consequently, fear would control the people for the duration of their occupation.

We were separated from the group to a little ravine where all could see. The rebel pointed his M-16 rifle at us and prepared to open fire. In the crowd were my mother and some of my siblings. She along with all the people that knew me began to cry and beg for my life seeking to assure this rebel I was not an enemy fighter. Escaping that moment in my life was absolutely a miracle of God noting the reputation of rebel soldiers and the importance of their need to make an emphatic arrival and statement to a conquered area.

Because of my athletic body and six-foot four-inch height, the threat didn't stop there. The word got out to area rebel commanders that there was a great conscript in the area. Through friends, the news reached me that rebel commanders were debating and betting on who would get me to join their group first. My mother tried her best to keep me out of sight of the rebels. As I was walking not far from my house a few days later, I ran into one of the rebel commanders and his crew. He called me over to where he was standing and asked me why I hadn't taken an AK-47 rifle yet to fight with them. I informed him that I was not interested in fighting. He proceeded to make me perform physically difficult exercises for a good long while to break my will into succumbing to his request. He used his pistol to shoot over my head and through my legs to intimidate me. He informed me that he knew I was a good basketball player, and since I didn't want to join him, he would shoot out my knees so that I had no future in the sport. Noting the situation, I maintained with as stern words as I could muster that I could not take up an AK-47 rifle. He eventually let me leave after a while but promised to continue to pressure me, and he did.

To guarantee saving your life, would you have compromised and taken an AK-47 rifle?

Courage to Obey Under Pressure

Due to the lack of opposition because of mass army deserters, rebels from the rural border areas had made a sudden descent on the capital city. At this time my sister was separated some fifty miles from the family. Between us multiple bloodthirsty warring factions occupied the territory. All of these factions were committing atrocities such as senseless and ritualistic killings, lootings, rapes, and so forth. Before the situation really heated up in the capital city, my dad had an opportunity to take the rest of his family out of the country to safety via an aircraft. He approached God in prayer for discernment. The Lord's continuous tug on his heart was his answer to not leave without his daughter and complete family. So he chose to keep the family in the midst of chaos and wait for his missing daughter to come home.

My sister, in the midst of starvation and displacement in a refugee camp, had a dream during which she spoke to my dad and received instruction to come home. It wasn't just that simple a dream however. In her dream, she was lying on her bedroom floor of my mom and dad's home when my dad walked into the room and told her, "Come home. We are waiting for you." As a result, she got the unwavering courage to take what little belongings she had, told the group she was with goodbye, and decided to walk home to find her family. Noting the distance she had to walk and her physical condition due to lack of food and proper resources, she absolutely shouldn't have made the choice. But she did. Worse than that, no one in their right mind, especially as a lonely female, walks through enemy zones of up to four warring factions engaged in guerilla warfare and expects to live or not see harm done to them. It took her two weeks of travel time on foot, seeking safety and sources she could trust, gruesome searches for food, as well as the doubts and fears that confronted her concerning accomplishing her goal, for her to complete the journey. A feat such as this can only be done if God has spoken words of conviction that cannot be rejected.

I was sitting on the front porch of our home when a young boy whom I recognized walked up with my sister, but I did not recognize her. My sister was also a healthy and strong athlete prior to the war. Starvation and dehydration had taken away all her stature, and I honestly could not identify her. It wasn't until she called my name as she collapsed to the ground that I saw who she was. Her body reacted to the relief of completing her journey in a strange way because she instantly began to vomit. Mind you, we are talking about an incredibly starved woman. If my dad had put his family on that aircraft, what I saw in that moment told me that the disappointment alone of not finding us at home when she arrived would have killed my sister. My dad gave me a couple of the greatest lessons of my life that day. The lessons learned are:

1) *Always, always take difficult and overbearing decisions to God, if not every decision.*
2) *Never usurp God's answer to your prayer with your desire for comfort or safety.*

As we continued in the struggle of doing what was necessary for survival in the war, my father and my family would soon find ourselves betrayed by a fellow we didn't hesitate to help when he was in need. Because rebels would unquestionably take food that didn't belong to them, we disguised the storage area where we kept a considerable amount of food to feed several families. One morning we awoke to rebels forcing us to take nothing and leave our home immediately as they stood with AK-47 rifles at our backs. The campus was quickly becoming the battlefront as one of the warring factions pushed to secure a buffer zone and prevent attacks on the capital city with rebel missiles coming from our area. As we fled, this individual whom we fed as a starving stranger for several months prior proceeded to inform the rebels of our disguised storage which had dwindled significantly by this time. Angry rebels began to conduct a manhunt for us, labeling my father a traitor and non-supportive of their cause. Sadly we didn't know the search was being conducted. I believe it was a blessing we didn't know because we probably would have tried to get away from the area and gravely aggravate the situation with an appearance of guilt.

We found ourselves displaced and homeless sitting in a hut in a village when two trucks of rebel soldiers came rolling in. Following an unforgettable turn of events which I describe later in this book, my father was carried away to be executed. Fortunately it was by order of a commander who wasn't present at the time of the arrest so he wasn't executed on the spot. Although several rebels (masquerading as kind men) came by and told us my father had been executed, he was held in a holding cell for a couple of days as commanders argued over why they were killing him. Guerilla warfare keeps no prisoners of war so this was greatly unusual when it came to the track record of the rebels. They decided to execute him and took him to the edge of a cliff to do so. He told us he looked down at the bottom of the cliff and saw countless numbers of dead people. His final prayer in preparation to join those that had gone before him was "Lord, all of those bodies were Your children as I am. So, if this is Your will I am ready." A spirit of fear gripped the rebel who was picked to do the execution, and he was incapable of pulling the trigger and completing the execution. My dad was unaware this happened and could not understand why he was left standing there for a while. They later took my dad back to his holding cell without explanation.

That evening he overheard a voice speaking and asking the rebel on duty if the old man with grey hair was still in the cell. The voice went on to explain that he tried to execute the old man but something scared him terribly. The rebels frequently engaged in cannibalism and ritualistic killings in order to earn demonic powers in battle. He felt something supernatural, but I assure you it wasn't demonic. It was a holy God. The word spread among the rebels, and as we were on the run to stay out of the range of mortars and bullets, rebels who met my dad would frequently ask if they could pay him for some of his power.

College Life, Basketball, and Racism

Let's fast-forward a couple of years. Through a window of a very brief cease-fire between warring factions, I was extremely fortunate to take advantage of a scholarship offer from a United States college. I left the rest of my family in the midst of the civil war that would last a total of fourteen years. I found myself in the middle of Coeur d'Alene, Idaho, and attending North Idaho College (NIC). Regardless of many incredible friends I made there and many wonderful memories of the city, it is ironic and humorous that God took me out of a hostile environment and into more hostility with the existence of the KKK (Ku Klux Klan). My wife and I share an extremely sentimental connection to the city of Coeur d'Alene. We met there at NIC, moved away to further our education and careers, but had our wedding ceremony in Coeur d'Alene because it is that magical a place for us. Nevertheless, racism was always around the corner or a dark street away.

I remembered once when a friend's son wanted to visit with me since I was an athlete at the college. His mother asked me to ride with her as she went to pick him up from school. As we drove by the high walls of what seemed to be a compound of some type, she proceeded to ask me if I knew or recognized the area. I said no. She nonchalantly said, "Oh, this is Hayden Lake, and that is the compound walls of the KKK." Why she would take me out there, and so dangerously close to the place was beside me. Armed guards shot at people of the wrong color while anywhere in the vicinity of that compound. Although there were physical racist attacks on people that I knew, fortunately the worst of my experience was being called *nigger* by unidentifiable parties at night. Elements of the group sought out dark streets where I happened to be and would drive by in their cars, turn off the lamps so I couldn't see who it was, scream obscenities, and speed off in a hurry.

Although my academic performance was stellar, these were trying and frustrating times for me on the basketball court. I wasn't getting any form of consistent playing opportunity on the court. My first year was a bit of a struggle as I fought to learn the more organized and structured systems of college basketball in America as opposed to Africa. Many of my friends and teammates saw my potential and thought I should have seen more opportunities to play. Some even urged me to transfer to a different school for fear of wasting precious time. I spoke to my coach and seemingly received a promise of more consistency the following year. Although I would seldom get used in spots to spark defensive and rebounding intensity, a full second year was wasted on the bench. With no official or quantifiable statistics to show would-be recruiters of a junior college athlete for the next level, I was spotted while playing in a spring tournament against several area NCAA Division I and ex-professional players and doing well to show my ability. A coach inquired of the friend and booster who brought me (and two other teammates who already had NCAA Division I offers) to the tournament and found out my situation. By the following weekend I was out on a recruiting trip to Montana Tech and eventually received a wonderful scholarship offer to play at an excellent academic institution from Coach Rick Dessing. In two years of consistent playing, I graduated with all-academic and all-American athletic honors.

The challenges never stopped coming as racism also appeared during my wonderful two and a half-year stay in Montana. This is quite close to the harshest personal attack of racism I endured. The woman who is my lovely wife now (but girlfriend then) was refused a rental house that she had already signed contracts for along with her roommates when the landlord noticed that she was dating a black man. My wife is obviously a Caucasian woman. I was helping her move her stuff in and had taken a load of her belongings into the house when he saw me enter. While I was indoors, he called her into his primary residence which was next door and vehemently attacked her verbally for bringing a "nigger" into his house. I came out looking for her. As I walked the streets, I noticed her silhouette in the house with him screaming at her. As I rushed to the door to defend her, she came running out with tears in her eyes and asked that we please leave immediately. She was unable to verbally express what was going on, but I could tell. It took all of her urging, and all of my thoughts of what the consequences would be for me had I reacted the way I wanted to, not to go in and retaliate physically that day.

What would you have done that day? Completed what I left undone by physically retaliating as I wanted to or maybe left the town in protest loud enough for the world to know?

Marriage or the Responsibility

When I left home and embarked on the trip to the United States for school, you will recall that I left my family in the midst of a treacherous civil war on the West Coast of Africa. That departure from my family signified a tremendous milestone and burden on my life. It was the day that my father bestowed on me the full responsibility of restoring the family noting the devastating setback that two years of the war had already imposed. My parents lost absolutely everything they had worked for and earned in close to thirty years of uncompromising service and complete dedication to a foreign country. I had five people (my sister, two younger brothers, mom and dad), not counting the adopted siblings yet, who were looking to me to deliver on the task of bringing hope to life once more. There was no option for failure on this task, and that was so deeply entrenched in me due to the struggles we had endured together as a family. Honestly, I don't believe I realize how deep until I got married.

I took an incredible woman for my partner and wife till death do us part. However, it became apparent that I was more married to my responsibility and family in Africa than I was her. I am not perfect by any stretch of the imagination, but at anytime of my life I have never been one to have a collection of addictive bad habits (drinking, drugs, womanizing, material things, and so on) of any kind. My only pursuit and addiction, if I may call it that, was the desire to restore my family and accomplish the task bestowed upon me by my father. I found it hard to understand why my wife could not see the necessity of the matter. She saw it quite well and even embraced it initially until I proceeded to abuse her commitment and trust.

I had an incredibly noble pursuit and well-packaged story to tell that would send chills up the back of the abominable snowman. However, my approach was terribly wrong. The order of priority when it came to the items of importance in my life was incredibly misplaced. My wife *may* have been the fourth or fifth important cause or concern in my life at that time. Sadly, God wasn't really in the picture (as a serious personal commitment) yet to demand a ranking. It took a toll on our marriage to the point of utter destruction to our lives, and that finally called me to attention. We separated, and my wife moved out of the home and in with a friend as we prepared for divorce.

Do you hate your marriage? If so, how much? Do you feel you have done so much damage to your marriage that it is absolutely unsalvageable?

What Is This Book All About?

Stop for a second and think...! Which one of these situations would have eventually been your downfall? Would any of these challenges have caused you to forfeit your role as a firstborn son? As a father or mother, especially a single mother or father, guardian or grandparent, or a mentor, are the children you are raising, specifically firstborn sons, prepared to face any and all of these challenges successfully? They have to be because all it takes is one failure to render him a life of doom and failure. Our society isn't in the business of doing us favors as parents; on the contrary it is robbing us and taunting us with blatant disregard in the process. More and more we see the erosion of the family and its value structures in the name of progressive thinking. Single-parent homes or absentee parenting is more of a proud acceptance and encouraged more now than ever before. Women are proud to say they no longer need a man as a partner in the home when it comes to raising children, especially aggressive and adventurous boys. Take a look at the results we are generating.

The following are taken from Single Parent Success Foundation:

- Births to unmarried women constituted 36 percent of all births in 2004, reaching a record high of nearly 1.5 million births. Over half of births to women in their early twenties and nearly 30 percent of births to women ages 25-29 were to unmarried women.

  "America's Children: Key National Indicators of Well-being, 2006" www.childstats.gov

- Along with the number of births to unmarried women, the birth rate for unmarried women rose in 2004. The 2004 rate of 46 births per 1,000 unmarried women ages 15-44 matches the historic high reported a decade earlier, in 1994

  "America's Children: Key National Indicators of Well-being, 2006" www.childstats.gov

- Between 1980 and 1994, the birth rate for unmarried women ages 15-44 increased from 29 to 46 per 1,000. Between 1995 and 2003, the rate has fluctuated little, ranging from 43 to 45 per1,000

"America's Children: Key National Indicators of Well-being, 2006" www.childstats.gov

- In 1995, nearly six of 10 children living with mothers only were near the poverty line. About 45 percent of children raised by divorced mothers and 69 percent by never-married mothers lived in or near poverty, which was $13,003 for a family of three in 1998.

Census Brief CENBR/97-1, Bureau of the Census www.census.gov, September 1997.

- 75% of children/adolescents in chemical dependency hospitals are from single-parent families.

(Center for Disease Control, Atlanta, GA)

- More than one half of all youths incarcerated for criminal acts lived in one-parent families when they were children.

(Children's Defense Fund)

- 63% of suicides are individuals from single parent families

(FBI Law Enforcement Bulletin - Investigative Aid)

- 75% of teenage pregnancies are adolescents from single parent homes

(Children in need: Investment Strategies...Committee for Economic Development) [1]

The following are taken from Childstats.gov, Forum on Child and Family Statistics.

- In 2008, 67 percent of children ages 0–17 lived with two married parents, down from 77 percent in 1980.

- In 2008, 23 percent of children lived with only their mothers, 4 percent lived with only their fathers, and 4 percent lived with neither of their parents.

- In 2008, 75 percent of White, non-Hispanic, 64 percent of Hispanic, and 35 percent of Black children lived with two married parents.

- The proportion of Hispanic children living with two married parents decreased from 75 percent in 1980 to 64 percent in 2008.

- Due to improved measurement, it is now possible to identify children living with two parents who are not married to each other. Three percent of all children lived with two unmarried parents in 2008. [2]

- There were 53 births for every 1,000 unmarried women ages 15–44 in 2007.

- Between 1980 and 1994, the birth rate for unmarried women ages 15–44 increased from 29 to 46 per 1,000. Between 1995 and 2002, the rate fluctuated little, ranging from 43 to 44 per 1,000; from 2002 to 2007, however, the rate increased from 44 to 53 per 1,000.

- Rates in 2006 remained highest for women ages 20–24 (79.5 per 1,000), followed closely by the rate for women ages 25–29 (74.9 per 1,000). [3]

- In 2007, 18 percent of all children ages 0–17 lived in poverty, an increase from 17 percent in 2006. Compared with White, non-Hispanic children, the poverty rate was higher for Black children and for Hispanic children. In 2007, 10 percent of White, non-Hispanic children, 35 percent of Black children, and 29 percent of Hispanic children lived in poverty.

- The poverty rate for children living in female-householder families (no spouse present) also fluctuated between 1980 and 1994; it then declined between 1994 and 2000 by more than the decline in the poverty rate for all children in families. In 1994, 53 percent of children living in female-householder families were living in poverty; by 2007, this proportion was 43 percent.

- Children in married-couple families were less likely to live in poverty than children living in female-householder families. In 2007, 9 percent of children in married-couple families were living in poverty, compared with 43 percent in female-householder families. [4]

- For 10th- and 12th-grade students in 2008, the percentage of White and Hispanic students who were heavy drinkers was approximately double the percentage of Black students. The percentages of 10th-grade White, Hispanic, and Black students who were heavy drinkers were 20, 20, and 10 percent, respectively. The percentages of White, Hispanic, and Black 12th-graders who were heavy drinkers were 30, 22, and 11 percent, respectively. Among 8th-grade students, the rate of heavy drinking was 8 percent for White, 12 percent for Hispanic, and 6 percent for Black students. [5]

- In 2007, 48 percent of high school students reported ever having had sexual intercourse.

- The proportion of students who reported ever having had sexual intercourse declined significantly from 1991 (54 percent) to 2001 (46 percent) and has remained relatively stable from 2001 to 2007.

- The percentage of students who reported ever having had sexual intercourse differs by grade. In 2007, 33 percent of 9th-grade students reported ever having had sexual intercourse, compared with 65 percent of 12th-grade students.

- Trends differed by race and ethnicity. The percentage of White, non-Hispanic students who reported ever having had sexual intercourse declined from 50 percent in 1991 to 43 percent in 2001, and remained between 42 percent and 44 percent from 2003 to 2007. This rate also declined among Black, non-Hispanic students, from 82 percent in 1991 to 67 percent in 2003, and remained between 67 percent and 68 percent from 2003 to 2007. There was no statistically significant change among Hispanic students between 1991 and 2007 (when the proportion was 52 percent).

- Overall, rates of sexual intercourse did not differ by gender, though they did differ by gender within some racial and ethnic groups. In 2007, 73 percent of Black, non-Hispanic male students reported ever having had sexual intercourse, compared with 61 percent of Black, non-Hispanic female students, and 58 percent of Hispanic male students reported ever having had sexual intercourse, compared with 46 percent of Hispanic female students. [6]

Now that we have taken a moment to read these statistics and get a clear view into the state of affairs of our communities and society, it is obvious that this is more than a race or just a single-parent issue. Our society is a direct reflection of what we as parents are sending out of our homes. As an African male, very frequently considered an African-American, I am sensitive to the staggering numbers put forth by blacks especially in the area of single-parent mothers. The evidence is incredibly more prominent in the lives of our inner-city youths. As a youth basketball coach, I see it all too often. These mothers often feel they have no choice or hope in the matter. Mothers, your sons have an awesome father in the person of God the Father, and He never leaves. Use this book to teach you how to break the vicious cycle that so dominantly defeats us. Send your sons out of your homes with principles that will train them to navigate this treacherous society as heroes, rather than be victimized into thinking anything less. This book has a very bold intention; it is to shock an already crippling and irregularly beating heart of our society and our families with a mental AED (Automatic Electronic Defibrillator) back to perfect rhythm.

The book focuses on the role of the firstborn son because I am convinced that a uniquely strategic role in this battle lies in the hands of the individuals who bear that title. If parents are able to reach and impart to their firstborn son a godly and long lasting family legacy, they begin an incredible trickle down effect. The firstborn immediately begins to affect his younger siblings who look up to and adore his every move both consciously and subconsciously. He is soon to become a man and not only affect those he comes into contact with and influences but also pass on that legacy to the next generation as a husband and father (high priest of his home). I believe this book will portray for you, beginning with my life, the same manner in which selfish men have led our homes and society into chaos, noble and sacrificial God-fearing men can restore our homes to a place of tranquility.

What Then Is a Firstborn Son?

A firstborn son is a legacy bearer, a protector, one who passionately embraces responsibility for others, one who endures hardship with resilience and integrity, and finally he pursues godly wisdom with vigor. God has had an extremely important place in His kingdom for the firstborn son. The Bible speaks of

Jesus Christ as the Firstborn amongst many brethren. As you read this book, you will learn of other key references in the Bible that you may not have known of. I believe we have hurt our society by mercilessly killing what was once honorably passed down for ages with great success. My father raised me with full awareness of my role as his firstborn son, and you have had a taste (earlier in the chapter) of how immeasurably well those principles served my choices in critical moments. The more I confront the selfish nature with which men approach life's difficulties, the more apparent the need to revive the virtues of this role within our culture. Don't be afraid if you don't have or aren't a firstborn son, the principles are quite transferable. They are just uniquely more powerful when applied to the life of a firstborn son.

This book reaches out to all facets of the family. It touches parents, siblings, sons and daughters, extended family, and friends. It also touches concepts of gifting, purposeful living, responsibility and commitment, building a circle of influence, cultural indicators and misrepresentations, marriage and the spousal selection process, marital restoration, mentoring and coaching, decision making, and more. Are you a father who is afraid your beautiful daughter is marrying a young man you feel isn't what you envisioned as a son-in-law? Do you realize that you are in the position to have a fatherly influence on his life and subsequently your grandchildren and generations to come rather than bring misery to his home? This book provides key principles to that effect. However, here is the key that brings it all together:

> "We demolish arguments and *every* pretension that sets itself up against the knowledge of God, and we take *captive every thought* to make it obedient to Christ" (2 Cor. 10:5, italics mine).

None of these unique and thought-provoking principles interlock and work in unison as they should unless they are in submission to the knowledge and lordship of Jesus Christ. If you attempt to burrow these principles without full submission to the inerrant Scriptures of the Holy Bible, I guarantee you a world of frustration and confusion. You will see the proof in the book as it speaks clearly for itself. It was not until I brought my life and that of my home into full submission of the Scriptures that the unity of these principles aligned themselves so beautifully. Challenges do come. But with Christ at the helm, I am, and we are, prepared.

CHAPTER TWO:

My Story, the African Beginnings

My parents moved to Liberia, West Africa, in the 1960s as African missionaries and teachers from the country of Cameroon in Central Africa. I am the firstborn son of four children born to my parents. Be careful now, because I said firstborn son. If you make a mistake and say firstborn child, I am not taking the whipping from my sister, you are. The oldest child is Rosalie, a girl, who is about six years older than I am. Then there is Oscar and Alexandre, three and six years younger than I am respectively. My parents were keen to raise all of their children to absolutely high standards. That is still evident today by the lives that each of us leads with regards to family commitments, marriage, children, and so forth. But I believe my parents decided to add a little extra spice and cooking to my preparation. I am going to spend time describing the environment of my upbringing. I believe it is critical to my life's later influences and my decision making as a firstborn son.

My parents chose to raise us kids on the campus of a Baptist boarding school. Since my parents were teachers there, I attended that school from kindergarten through my graduation from high school. The school had a heavy religious affiliation and had a partnership with the Southern Baptist Convention of the USA. There was a high level of foreign teachers as well, so the influence of the community was highly diverse. School instructors in my upbringing (from what I remember) were from countries such as Ghana, Sierra Leone, Togo, India, Cameroon, France, Nigeria, Liberia, and America. The auditorium of the school doubled as our church known as Washington Chapel Baptist Church. Those Christian and spiritual ties were deeply entrenched in the occurrences of everyday living on the campus.

Early before the beginning of every school day, students and faculty would begin the day in the auditorium of the school for a thirty-minute devotional time before heading to classes. Part of the curriculum at every grade level included a Bible education class in addition to the sciences, literature, and other social studies. Every evening, following afternoon extra-curriculum activities such as sports and other events, the students had an evening devotion time before breaking for study hall, homework, and so on.

The Sunday activities also found students in proper uniform attire of all white dresses with black shoes for girls, and black pants, white, long-sleeved shirts, and black neckties for boys. At first there would be Sunday school, worship service, and later additional youth events like RA (Royal Ambassadors) as governance of the early morning activities. Sunday evenings also had a mandatory evening shorter worship service.

As you can probably tell by now, academics and spirituality were inseparable for much of my upbringing. There is no doubt in my mind that the narrow roadmap and the lifestyle or ideology I will describe many times in this book was gained in these walls. These were regimented academic and spiritual confines that engulfed me during those early and greatly influential years of my life. They provided me an incredible foundational understanding of what my belief and values were to be as I became an adult.

If you find as you read this book that you admire mine or my family's response to adversity, or the resurgence and resilience after a fall, I would encourage you to consider the environment in which you have your family or children. That environment greatly impacts their future choices and responses in life. Environment doesn't necessarily refer to the city you live in, but more importantly the people, teachings, and sources impacting their and your lives. No matter what the situation, you control that decision to change your environment or stay there. I confidently attest that God can bring greatness out of every situation if we allow Him to influence our choices.

Physical Environment

Liberia is located on the Atlantic coastline of West Africa. Except for dense forests along the way, we were no more than five to ten miles from the ocean shore. The campus itself, although sprinkled nicely with concrete structures that served as living quarters for instructors, dormitories, clinic, cafeteria, workshops, and administrative buildings, was quite populated with palm trees and fruit trees of all kinds. Not too far behind my house was a creek that allowed me to hone my day and night fishing skills as a boy with trips my dad, brothers, and I took. At other times, I was chasing squirrels and birds with my sling shots to keep myself busy, if I wasn't raiding some fruit trees or watermelon patch. There was always something to do and the lures of drugs and alcohol or violence were not attractive, although I new drinkers, drug users, and thieves.

The campus was its own little settlement in terms of the hotbed of activities that occurred all around. Several villages, with traditional primitive African housing surrounded the campus up to a ten-mile radius. Because of the medical, spiritual, employment, and certainly academic benefits, the school entertained scores of individuals from around the area. Many of my friends happened to reside in these villages and other surrounding areas. Many of my parents' friends happened to be these people as well. My dad was an administrator and professor at the school. He was also an avid hunter. He would walk for long periods of time hunting the bushes of the area for miles and miles from where we lived. But that also meant he knew the surrounding areas and villages very well, including its inhabitants. That personal attribute of my dad's would come in extremely handy later on in life as war ravaged our home and community. Those people, being so fond of my dad, greatly accommodated us when we found ourselves displaced and homeless because of the fighting and rebels desperate to loot our home. More importantly, my father exhibited incredible people skills that I observed firsthand, and it has shaped my thinking and impressed on me the embrace of a similar approach

Academic Expectations

My mother taught kindergarten for over twenty-five years. She was an extremely hard worker as an educator. She also superbly filled the role of the African housewife who was to ensure the house was spotless, as well as having a fully prepared warm meal for her large family (at anytime included four or more adopted children) three times a day. I am not sure how she did it, but because of that she did not cut us kids any slack on sniffing laziness. *(Take note here, single mothers, it can be done, and you can be a beacon for your son, a legendary champion in his eyes. I am confident that with the luxuries and amenities we have at our disposal these days, you are not busier than my mother was.)* My mother was also my kindergarten teacher, and she did a superb job of preparing her pupils annually. They say that the preparation of the child in the kindergarten year builds the aptitude and ability for learning that follows in the rest of academia. I haven't done the research, and I don't know how true that is, but I got a tremendous foundation from my mother as my kindergarten teacher. Her pupils frequently showed incredible readiness by the time they entered the elementary education system.

I was always academically good in school. I was a primarily straight A student with an expected ranking of no less than second in my class right on from elementary through high school. So my parents set the bar high to match my aptitude for academic development. I also enjoyed just about every activity I could get my hands on. As a result, I participated in events such as choir, band, musical quartet, basketball (school and club), Royal Ambassadors (youth ministry), social activities director, sound check technician, interscholastic competitive quizzing team, and anything else that needed a warm body it seems. My parents never stopped me from doing any of these things, but they new that my first love was basketball. So, if any of my grades ever dropped to a C+, I was grounded primarily from basketball for next six-week period until I restored that grade. So that taught me I didn't have the option to mess up, even slightly.

I remember once when I played the fool in mockery of my literature instructor knowing I couldn't fail her class. I produced a

D on my final exam. As a sophomore in high school I was beginning to earn great exposure for my basketball ability. This is similar to the kind of exposure kids would get from college recruiters or the AAU circuit in the USA and it carried heavy importance. A local club came to speak to my father about letting me play for their team that summer (school was done for the year), and he said no because of my exam grade. It was not because of my annual performance. I was still top of my class. I tried to claim it was a single exam as many young teenage men, and adults surprisingly would justify, but no, not nearly. He did it because he saw an attitude that he had to adjust immediately and not let it blossom. My father's decision hurt me to the core and scared me straight for sure.

I mention the academic expectations of my parents toward me because this is one of the areas in my life that I received some of the greatest molding as a person and firstborn son. It was never an even playing field. My siblings, although they were capable, didn't seem to be pushed that hard. I believe my sister was pushed a bit where my dad, as her instructor, would refuse to answer any class questions at home, since her classmates didn't have the luxury of having the teacher at home as she did. But I don't remember any of the other siblings, or adopted kids, being grounded for academics the way I was. It felt like it was such a hard and unfair expectation that I literally decided to rebel during my junior year of high school and not apply myself to dominance of the class rankings. I also felt that my mother frequently compared me to my rivals and a few other students in other classes. I just decided I could care less about the results. I didn't stop succeeding in school; I just didn't care what ranking I took. The consequence for my actions was missing the valedictorian position at graduation by a tiny fraction of a point. It was not until quite a few years later, in my adulthood that my mother acknowledged that those kids she compared me to did not participate in nearly the amount of activities with which I was involved. That was probably about the greatest compliment or acknowledgement I could have received from my mother.

My school as a whole, but more specifically the high school, had a reputation for being one of the top five schools in the country over the years and still holds that honor to this day. It was and is arguably the best school in the country. The educational curriculum of the country also required that at the freshmen and senior year, national exams were administered. Subject matters testing included the sciences, English literature, mathematics, and social studies. If a student did not pass all the subjects of this examination, he or she could not be promoted to the next grade level. The success rate of its students was usually a great indication of the schools excellence.

I believe there was a greater measure to the excellence in education my school provided. Without any experience in the education system of American high schools, I was asked to take the SAT in the beginning of my pursuit to attend university in the United States. I was prepared adequately to pass that and qualify for many schools or universities in America at the NCAA level and below.

Basketball—My and My Family's God-Sent Redemption

As a young kid, pre-teen years especially, during the school year I had many friends to play and hang out with. When school was over with for the summer and kids went home to see their parents, there were not many in the way of bodies my age to play or socialize with. Early on, my two younger brothers were really little, therefore there was not much to identify with being three and six years apart respectively.

So, although much of Africa, including Liberia, predominantly plays soccer my school happened to garner more notoriety for basketball athletically. As my father and I would go into town and into a particular supermarket, they had these truly unofficial weight basketballs for sale. At that time, I could care less about official weight since I knew no better. I would frequently ask, and he finally obliged and bought me the ball. My house was about two hundred yards away from the school's concrete basketball court. My mother could watch me all day and knew I was safe. I would go and play for hours everyday during the summers. My boarding student friends from the dormitories were all gone and every once in a while a friend from the surrounding village would come by. I worked on all facets of the game I could think of. The older kids, and some nationally influential ball players that were students of my school but played for a city club team, would sometimes ask to use the court for practices. That was a great opportunity to sit on the side of the court and watch the older fellows play. That was greatly educational, and I would go out and work on what I had seen. These were my elementary years.

I eventually asked my dad if I could be somewhat of a team manager, only for the basketball team obviously, through my elementary and early junior high years. He allowed me to do so, and I got to watch the games firsthand and close up. Then I went back during those many lonely hours and worked on what I saw. There was no youth basketball developmental programs or camps to attend. There was one coach that took additional interest in helping me develop when I was finally old enough to go into the city on my own by taxi. My desire was to go to the local YMCA on Saturday mornings and play with some competition for a few hours.

There was also one phenomenal player from a local village named Cooper Gaye. Cooper's family was so poor that they could not afford to put him through school, much less buy him a single pair of shoes. He would come out and play with the kids during the school year. He played on concrete with his bare feet and was still practically unstoppable, a great shooter. But he was aware of his immense poverty and could not work up the nerve to accept the lures to play in the city with the bigger teams. He tried but never felt like he fit. Well I wasn't a threat to his condition so Cooper and I ended up playing countless numbers of one-on-one games. I have to admit that we played each other for several years. Like an older brother, he'd beat me without mercy. Then the day finally came when I beat him and realized in my own little way, I had arrived. To beat Cooper, who even the best and older players in the city feared, was incredible.

I remember the confidence that came over me as my skill and physical abilities (my vertical jump and more) elevated. My freshmen year came by and I made my school's varsity basketball squad, and I honestly can't remember anyone that did so during my time at the school. As the students came back to school that year, and we all rushed to the court to play, I was quickly dubbed the nickname Mt. Cameroon (my parental heritage). I was blocking shots incredibly well and dunking easily as well. It was no doubt I had been spotted.

Staying on basketball's good fortune for my life, fast-forward to my graduation from high school and my plans to begin studies at the University of Liberia. There were only two major higher learning universities in the country. I was one of only two high school players, with several hundred schools in the country, offered an athletic scholarship to the University of Liberia for basketball. The other was a well-known specimen of an athlete that graduated from a basketball powerhouse (St. Patrick's High School) by the name of Kollie Zayzay. That offer usually meant you had an automatic usher into the country's national team and further exposure to the international play. I never got to experience any of that due to the Liberian civil war. Unfortunately, the rumors of war began to circulate throughout the country the day I graduated from high school in 1989, and the war began on Christmas Eve, two days later.

I write about my basketball progression as a young athlete in Liberia to give you a picture or example of how God can use anything and anywhere He desires to mold the talent or tool He has chosen to accomplish His task through you. Earlier I mentioned that my parents were not terribly thrilled I spent so much time on the court. They were simply not fully aware that God was developing a gift that would serve a specific purpose for us all. In my case, I didn't need world renowned youth coaches, camps, or leagues. He just put in me a desire and love for the game and brought a Cooper Gaye that was an elusive target I had to pursue for years, which forced me to strive harder and harder. All of this happened in a country where 99 percent of children, particularly boys, prefer to play soccer and could care less about basketball.

A Miraculous God Is Always Present

I know the plan I have for you…said the Lord (see Jeremiah 29:11). My parents observed how much time I put into learning this game. They would always say, "Sports doesn't pay in Africa. Go and focus on your academics." In the era that I grew up, my parents were absolutely right concerning Africa. But God was thankfully bigger than Africa. Sports didn't pay in Africa, but it paid a great deal for my schooling in the USA and for getting my family to America and allowing me to accomplish the mission my father and mother set before me when I left home. That mission was to study hard and get us out of the significant setback and reality the Liberian civil war had draped upon us. My parents and our family, due to the war, had lost everything (possessions, finances, and much more) they had worked for in close to thirty years of uncompromising service in Liberia. It was all gone except for God's wonderful gift of life. Yes, we were all still breathing regardless of many life-threatening situations. Praise God!

In this life, the acceptance of influential advice from the right people is priceless. During my senior year in high school, God brought Lloyd and Marjorie Garrison into my life. They came to Liberia for four months as volunteer Southern Baptist missionaries. Lloyd was filling in as the pastor of our church, and he also taught my comparative religion class.

Lloyd observed my success in the classroom and began to take a quiet interest. As mentioned earlier, I was heavily involved in music as a highly visible vocal choir performer and member of a national performing quartet of teenagers. I also served as a Sunday school teacher and youth ministry leader. I did just about everything that was needed with utmost attentiveness and maintained my position at the head of my class with a renewed desire to dominate the rankings unlike my junior year. Lloyd would also come daily and sit on the side of the basketball courts and watch us boys play, as well as observe the interaction and attitudes.

About a month before Lloyd and Marjorie were to return to the United States, they came over to my house to talk to my parents and me. They informed us that he had been watching me, and he thought I possessed all the tools to come to the USA for school and succeed. He said if we were interested, he was interested in coming to the United States and securing a scholarship for me.

I have to interject and tell you how great a man of faith Lloyd Garrison was (he has since passed on). Lloyd was an old Texan that moved his family to the northwestern United States without a whole lot of promise of material gain that man could offer. But he was amazingly influential in the planting of over twenty-five to thirty northwest churches throughout his years because his promise was from God. He would go out daily and knock on the doors of people in his community to genuinely tell them about the love of Christ and his desire to have them come and visit his church. I vividly remember his words to me, "Ezechiel, it is time to go visiting." And off we would go. That is how he built his church and the personalities and commitments he garnered were incredible. There were also stories of Lloyd walking into local bars and preaching to people he met there just as they were. Marjorie, as a supportive wife, wasn't any less impressive in her functions and her role. Lloyd took that same faith in his efforts and desires to help me.

Lloyd and Marjorie Garrison returned to the United States without even a simple video of me playing basketball. All he had was a cassette recording of me singing in various capacities and his testimony of my attitude and academic success. Soon after his return, I began to receive offer letters for basketball and musical scholarships from Baylor University and Wayland Baptist University out of Texas. I had begun to prepare to travel and take advantage of the opportunity immediately upon my graduation from high school. However, the civil war began in Liberia, West Africa. I lost all contacts with the universities and the Garrisons as no form of communication was available during the violence.

Two years later, I was finally able to make a call to inform the Garrisons I was still alive and interested in coming for school. A very volatile three-month cease-fire agreement had been reached between the warring parties. The international community had frequently called on the rebel factions to come to the dialogue table. The multi-country (West African) representation of a peace keeping force that was sent in to help was brutally attacked and became a fourth faction in this confusion. This was the only time I had to get out or lose this chance again very possibly forever. As a matter of fact, I left in the month of December and by April or

May of the following year, the talks broke down and the fighting that ensued practically lasted for the next ten plus years. That war virtually isolated the country of Liberia from the rest of the world except for weapons, drugs, and diamond smugglers.

The Garrisons at this time resided in Spirit Lake, Idaho. Lloyd walked into the office of a hall of fame basketball coach Roland "Rolly" Williams at North Idaho College in Coeur d'Alene, Idaho, to tell Rolly about this African kid he has without any video evidence to present. Lloyd asked for a scholarship.

I have to clearly paint the magnificent picture that this is and the incredible hand of God. Coach Williams was not hurting for players by any stretch of the imagination. Hall of fame coaches have players beating down their doors in this country when it comes to recruiting. Recruiting also requires countless kinds of scrutiny on videos and in person, as well as the opinions of coaches that player has competed for and against and so forth. Coach Williams truly and regularly had an amazing and athletic array of players and was an amazing recruiter regardless of his locale in a little town in northern Idaho. He recruited the world over, including the basketball hotbeds of the country like New York, California, Las Vegas, and others. My teams alone in two years at NIC, if I can describe, had six-foot four-inch- to seven-foot players from locations such as New York, California, New Jersey, Maryland, Chicago, Washington, DC, Holland, Brazil, The Bahamas, Australia, Canada, Bulgaria, and Liberia, which was me. As you can see, he had connections and no need for an undersized post player. He also had no need to listen to an old preacher who had no real background in the sport of basketball. But God had prepared his heart long before.

Coach Williams promised the Garrisons he would offer me a scholarship if they could get me to the United States. He did so without seeing a single video of what he was getting in terms of a player. That was a huge risk on his part to give away a scholarship. That was a lot of money not just for a full scholarship but more so for an international student. Have you checked the cost of tuition and requirements for international students lately? God had obviously prepared Coach Williams's heart long in advance.

I don't plan to go into too much specific details of my collegiate basketball career in this book. It too has many incidents of God molding me into the man that I am. I will just say this: I embraced the opportunities and experiences God gave me. The communities I was a part of embraced me wholeheartedly as well. My collegiate basketball career in the USA was a very successful one with many awards academically and athletically. I was fortunate to receive honorable mention All-American honors and more as an athlete. Now I strive to pass on what so many people have given me when they had no obligation to do so. I continue to follow the roadmap.

Firstborn son, I may not have millions of dollars in my bank account that came from the NBA. But I have an incredible rags-to-riches story that came from the incredible circle of influence that engulfed me with God's preparation, and it keeps on giving. It sometimes felt unfair, passion-filled, even seemed hopeless at times, and sometimes unbelievably timely with miraculous results. Are you content with where the Lord has you and are you willing to trust, accept, and embrace that His plan for you is unique and exclusive? I challenge you to do that.

As great as the sport of basketball has been to me and the miraculous way God used it in my life, I was nearly robbed of this gift by the fight for life through a treacherous war.

CHAPTER THREE:

The Liberian Civil War: A Fight for Life and Family

As briefly mentioned in the previous chapters, the Liberian civil war in essence aggressively pulled the rug out from under our family. I graduated from high school just a few short days before it started, and I was looking forward to a life of great promise. There was the opportunity to travel to the United States for college strongly developing. If that happened to fail, there was still excitement as I prepared to attend the University of Liberia with a strong prospect of a solid athletic career to aid me along the way. In my mind's limited eye, life was shaping up greatly. However, there was a weird rumor spreading like wild fire throughout the country.

The rumor said, "Out of the mouth of a newborn baby came these words, 'It is going to rain on Christmas Day, and anyone that the rain touches is going to die.'" Africans have long utilized fables passed down from generations orally to children to make a point or two when necessary. But strangely, this didn't sound like one of those fables. Well if you know anything about weather in Liberia, which is literally right on the equator, you know that there are two seasons. They are the rainy and dry season. It literally seems like it rains for six months and absolutely dries up for six months. Dry season means scorching heat that burns up the grass, and everything else it seems goes crispy brown and becomes fire ready. Christmas Day is literally about midway through the dry season, and there is absolutely no chance of rain during that time of the year. Furthermore, when was the last time a newborn baby spoke clearly? Well, it was a warning. It was a warning that on Christmas Day or there about a war would begin in the country. The "rain" the baby spoke of signified bullets. And if the bullets touched you, you would die.

There is a deeper longer story to the cause of the Liberian civil war. I will try to give you a very brief insight into the history for the sake of helping you understand the root of the atrocities. I assure you however, that I am absolutely not doing it justice in this book. That subject matter will honestly require a book of its own. The intent for discussing the war in this book is to share a broader light on my role as the firstborn son in my family and how this occurrence shaped my family and me. As a result, the discussion concerning the war will be more about incidents that occurred in my family and how we addressed them.

A Brief Insight to the Cause of the Liberian Civil War

In the year 1821, freed slaves in America, who were generally taken from the coasts of Africa, decided they wanted to return to Africa rather than remain free in the commonwealth. They embarked on this journey with the help of a group called the American Colonization Society. They were free, but the color of their skin still posed a big problem for them as residents in America. Some felt the best solution was to go back to Africa. So they did and settled on an island on the West Coast of Africa that they would call Perseverance. That also began the construction of a country they would later call Liberia.

Well for that settlement to rise there had to be a forceful dominance of a people that already existed on the land as natives. They surely had not sent out a letter of invitation for multiple ships of people and strangers to come and inhabit their lands. Well after scores of battles and death on both sides an agreement was reached for some form of coexistence. In 1847, Liberia declared its independence as a sovereign state with all of its leaders originating from the educated masses of the freed slaves community and their

American Colonization Society influence. Its first president was Joseph Jenkins Roberts.

Sadly, the freed slaves formed the ruling class of the country and practically suppressed the development of the natives and their descendants. The suppression was almost as much as the slavery they themselves had been subjected to in America. This state of affairs existed for over 130 years of the country's existence, although a bit milder in latter years, until a military rebellion ensued in 1980 that assassinated the then president Rev. Dr. William R. Tolbert and thirteen members of his political cabinet on Sugar Beach. Dr. Tolbert intended to remove the existence of animosity between the groups and unify the people as one, Liberians. In so doing, he alienated himself from the descendants of the freed slaves, his people, and could not fully win the trust of the natives which resulted in a military takeover.

Samuel Kanyon Doe, a master sargent in the army and a member of the Krahn tribe, assumed leadership of the ruling group that initially had several other native tribes represented. Within ten years of military rule, Doe had killed or forced into exile all the members of his sixteen-man team that led the rebellion. He also strategically surrounded himself, the government, and military leaders with people from his tribe to insure loyalty. Also within that ten-year period, it is said that there were over fifty assassination attempts on his life, all of which failed. In 1985, one attempt by an exiled member of his original team from 1980 came very close to success. Upon foiling this attempted takeover and assassination, Doe set out to practically commit genocide on the tribe of his enemy whom he had already caught and killed. Soldiers went up country into an area called Nimba County and ruthlessly killed defenseless men, women, and children. For those that survived, the area became the hottest recruiting ground for rebel leader Charles Taylor's hired attempt to perform a nation-sweeping massacre and Samuel Doe cornering all out civil war on Liberia. Quick assassination attempts had been wildly unsuccessful to say the least. And guess who were the ones primarily involved in the hiring? Descendants of freed slaves who wanted the seat of power back in their hands. That in a nutshell is how the rumor of a baby speaking and deadly rain falling on Christmas Day began.

"By justice a king gives a country stability, but one who is greedy for bribes tears it down" (Prov. 29:4).

The Liberian civil war started out of pure greed for power and indeed wealth by its leaders through the many years. Greed for power among leaders exists all over the world. Man is God's creation, and our sin whether in Africa, Europe, Asia, America, or wherever is not different or unique. In Liberia, it all just came to fruition with a nation-sweeping event that began in December of 1989. The greed then manifested itself into a tribal conflict for which all suffered. That tribal conflict very nearly turned into a religious conflict as the Mandingo tribe (primarily Islamic) aligned with the Krahn and was targeted by the Gio and Mano tribes of Nimba County. Later in the conflict, another warring faction that was financed by the Mandingos began their campaign for power and made a serious mark in the outcome of the war as well. I have laid out this little description to put forth a depiction that greed does indeed tear down. Greed is a sin, and sin leads to death both spiritually and physically as evidenced by the outcome in Liberia.

A Family Divided

Charles Taylor was a one-time student at my high school, Ricks Institute, but he was expelled. He also had dealings with my father when he arrived at Ricks Institute in the 1960s as a professor at the school. Taylor came into Nimba County and recruited young men who had absolute hate for Doe after the attempted genocide to start his war. Some of these young men were well focused on the job at hand they had been hired to do. (These men decided to break away from Taylor and commit to the task of getting to the capital city of Monrovia first and eliminate Samuel Doe.)

The majority of Taylor's recruits, however, were simply common thugs with automatic rifles in their hands and completely unfocused on the job at hand. They threatened, killed ruthlessly, raped, stole, and ravaged homes and communities. (Ironically they called themselves freedom fighters, but they were officially called the National Patriotic Front of Liberia, or NPFL.) Because Taylor's forces were distracted and uncommitted to the task, instead too focused on committing atrocities, it took the war about eight months to reach our campus. The rebels didn't have much resistance from the army whose members were quickly deserting their posts due to news of massive deaths by truckload ambushes. All sides were heavily involved in conscripting young men and child soldiers forcefully. That act destroyed far too many young lives and families and has also created incredible numbers of orphans. Sadly many of these orphans are children whose parents refuse to claim them for fear that they have been damaged by murderous acts they were forced to commit. Let me be clear that my siblings and I could have easily been victims with similar fates were it not for God's influence and preparation on our lives and family, as well as our obedience.

Allow me to give you a more detailed account of my sister, Rosalie's, separation from us at the time. Rosalie resided on the University of Liberia's science campus quite a few miles outside the city. Geographically describing this scenario, she was miles outside of the east end of the city, and we were miles outside of the west end of the city, approximately some fifty miles apart would be my guess. When the rebel forces laid siege to the city with attacks from multiple sides and multiple warring factions, we were completely disconnected from her. She happened to be in a displaced camp with friends. Savage rebel soldiers surrounded them, and there was no food since all relief sources had been cut off due to the fighting.

As a Cameroonian national, and as fighting in the country began to get treacherous, my dad had a very difficult decision to make. Cameroon had sent in a plane or two to extract its nationals. But since his daughter was not with the family he chose not to leave or separate the family until he had his daughter in tow. So we stayed in the midst of the chaos. My sister had no way of knowing if we had boarded the plane or just decided to walk to the neighboring border country of Sierra Leone to safety as so many others were doing.

My dad informed us that following his prayers, God was tugging on his heart to not leave the country without the entire family together. Miraculously, my sister had a dream during which she saw my father telling her to come home. As a result, she got the unwavering courage to take what little belongings she had, told her friends goodbye, and decided to walk home to find her family. Walking home as she did in a starved and dehydrated condition was harsh in itself, noting the distance. She told us of a gruesome and treacherous two-week period in which she had a soulful struggle to get back to her family. Walking as a lonely female through these zones with guerilla warfare erupting around her, she could have easily been falsely accused and killed for a variety of reasons.

Someone that knew our family and lived on the road by which she traveled home saw my sister's physical condition and asked their son to carry her bag for her. She was approximately five miles from home and could not carry it any more due to exhaustion. I happened to be sitting on the front porch when my sister walked up with this young boy. I saw this starved and dehydrated girl. I could not even identify her as my own sister. Rosalie had lost all stature. My beloved sister whom I had known all my life and a previously sturdy athlete, I absolutely could not recognize but for her familiar voice.

As a firstborn son, my father had just given me some of the many great examples of what it means to walk with God and make a difficult decision. He taught me what it means to stay the course of God's calling regardless of the lack of safety and comfort we may be faced with. I also learned how important it is to take every decision I am faced with to God. Firstborn son, we cannot usurp God's answer to our prayers regardless of how difficult it may seem with our craving for comfort. God uses the foolish things of this world to shame the wise and the weak things to shame the strong and mighty (see 1 Corinthians 1:18-31). The wisdom of God contradicts man's wisdom. Can you imagine what would have happened if we had indeed boarded that plane, or if my dad had not heeded the answer to his many prayers to not leave without his daughter? As I said before, I have no doubt my sister would have died out of disappointment alone.

Harassment and Being Tormented into Submission

Although my sister had encountered the rebels and the fighting up close and personal, the rebels had not yet seen the strategic need to take control of our area yet. They were just beginning to realize the need to constrict the city which then forced them to lay siege of our area which was west of the capital city Monrovia. They had been attacking from the east and the north, and the Atlantic Ocean was south. Day one of the rebels' arrival into our area, I became a target. The biggest controlling factor for a rebel force involved in guerilla warfare is to instill fear in the hearts of the people they oppress. As a result, when the rebels took over a new area, most likely someone had to die in order for them to set fear in the hearts of the people.

We were sitting home one afternoon as a family. The dormitories on the campus had been opened to thousands of displaced people fleeing fighting from all directions. Since the school had a female principal, my father decided to take the lead as a male and protect her from harassment. Someone came from one of the dormitories and informed us that there was a person rounding people up with a gun. My father took his gun (an avid hunter) and disappeared into the bushes to take a closer look at what was happening. We were not fully expecting these would-be rebels. Before long the rebels had rounded up the whole campus and had us all marching in one big group to the gated entrance of the campus. My father was nowhere to be found, and by this time we were not sure how many rebels were hiding in the bushes and out of site prepared to launch a counterattack if necessary. In other words, for all we knew, my father could have been dead, especially if found with a gun.

As we walked in a large group with hands held high and being herded by rebels with automatic weapons, I happened to catch up with a close friend who was displaced in one of the dormitories. Not really looking at each other noticeably, George, my friend, makes a comment to me, "Bambolo, trouble has arrived, and these guys are NPFL rebels." I make a short comment back. One of the rebels sees us talking and immediately accuses us of being enemy soldiers planning a counterattack on them. He separates us from the group and sends us down into a grassy ravine-type area within site of the rest of the people including friends, my family, but most especially, my mother. George (who was adopted) also has some family in the crowd, but he can't identify them because they are brothers and sons of a government senator. Nor do they dare identify themselves in his defense or try to come to his aid. That in itself is a written death note. As a matter of fact, they were forced to escape from the campus immediately as they began to notice many of the rebels were from the county and jurisdiction their father served as senator. There was no doubt someone would eventually recognize them. Unfortunately they would be noticed and arrested a few days later in their struggle to escape to safety. Their story of survival in that attempt to escape to safety is a miraculous one indeed, but God granted them favor.

The rebels had now selected George and me as their candidates to instill fear in the people. We were about to be executed in front of everybody including my mother. As one rebel trained his M-16 rifle on us, my mother screams in tears pleading that I am her son and not an enemy soldier. She tells him I am just a student at the university. He said there were many university students that were coming out to fight them. Then he proceeded to tell her that if she was my mother and she didn't want me to die, she could step in and take my place. She began to cry harder and pleaded my case to him. He showed no mercy. She told him that if he would truly guarantee that he would not kill me she would die in my place, but he gave no such guarantee. There were mothers of some of my friends in the crowd that reached out to console my mother and aid in the dialogue that lasted about five minutes. As he retrained his rifle to open fire, the whole crowd began to cry and scream that they know me, and I was not an enemy soldier. He is somewhat stunned by the reaction. He called us out of the ravine and warned us that he would keep a very close watch on us, and the slightest hint otherwise, he would execute us. We were able to escape death by the help of God, but it did not take long after the roundup that we began to find executed bodies and people who had been severely tied, beaten, and accused of being spies. Life had no real value in such conditions.

If you had something they wanted (food, clothing, money, and so forth) and refused to give it to them, they would kill you and take it. Years later I received sad news that although the day George and I stood in the ravine awaiting execution wasn't our appointed time to die, George did lose his life later during a rebel attack encounter.

Now that I had been spotted, a healthy-bodied athlete, the word got out to the commanders that there was a great candidate around to conscript. My friends began to tell me they heard commanders arguing about who was going get me into their rebel unit. They put the word out through some of the girls I knew that had been forced into relationships with the rebels. My mother heard about it and tried everything to keep me out of sight on the main streets. I stepped out close to my home one day to run an errand, and I unfortunately ran into one of the commanders and his unit unexpectedly. He summoned me and began to interrogate me on why I hadn't joined his unit. I told him I was not interested in fighting. He began to pop bullets just above my head and between my legs with his pistol. He went on to torment me with grueling physical exercises for a good long time in an attempt to break my will. He commented that he'd heard that I was a good basketball player, and if I didn't decide to join his unit, he would shoot out my knees, and I would have no future in the sport anymore. After a good while he decided to let me go and promised to come and find me again. He told me to think hard about picking up an AK-47 with him. The threat loomed for as long as the rebels were on the campus, almost two to three months. It was a comfortable place, and they really had no plans of leaving. In order to protect us boys, my father began to take us into the woods for all night fishing trips. He did this so that if the rebels came at night hunting to harass me and my father, they would not know where to find us.

Regardless of all of the harassment and torment, it never crossed my mind once to consider becoming a rebel. For one, I quickly discerned that their cause (freedom fighter?) was not just by any means. As a matter of fact, they were common thugs more interested in looting and pillaging to sell across the border with neighboring countries for money. The frequent disregard for life was all so clear. I saw executions occur in which accusation of the accused clearly did not add up. I saw deaths that occurred not by the bullet but instead by starvation and deterioration of health that sadly could not have been prevented due to the treacherous conditions. For lack of food and other threats, there were other friends of mine who justified carrying an automatic weapon. To some extent, that was the cool thing to do as a young man. You got the girls and power since you had an AK-47. Isn't that a similar draw in the street gangs of the inner cities or other restless areas of our world? Not for me, the roadmap did not instruct me as such. Contrary to that belief, it taught me to stand firm to values even in the presence of immediate danger. The apostle Paul and the disciples of Jesus Christ did just that numerous times. No one was a better example of such living than our Lord Jesus Christ Himself.

The last and probably most important factor that kept me from picking up a rifle was the knowledge that I had several young men and brothers looking up to me and watching closely. The moment I made such a decision, they were sure to follow. As the firstborn son, it was clear all along that where I led, they would follow. We were all at risk of death at any given moment, especially from the hands of a drugged up rebel. But we had to find food to stay alive. The boys in the family decided to embark on rallying together for projects to generate money and buy food as we ran about avoiding the fighting. Our primary source for finding money was chopping down trees with axes, as well as cutting them into four- to six-foot pieces to stack and burn to produce charcoal. Without electricity, since rebels had damaged such infrastructure, charcoal was in high demand primarily for cooking needs. Many times, the search to purchase food took us miles from where we slept at night, and that also meant the risky bush walk and avoidance of rebel soldiers at checkpoints who would most likely take the food for themselves. We kept a set of dogs with us which we would take hunting regularly to track down sources of meat for our balance in dietary consumption. We also fished local streams and rivers a lot for various kinds of fish. I have to admit, for a time of war and fear all about, as well as the day-to-day inconsistency of where life had us, these activities provided a lot of trust, growth, camaraderie, and simply a source of fun in the midst of all the hardships. It actually made the time go by faster. I thank God everyday for holding me close.

You Can Keep This One, the Rest We Will Kill

Since my father assumed the role of head administrator to protect the female principal, he took on the responsibility of assuring the well being of any faculty and staff left on campus. Just before the rebels took control of the campus, food was getting quite scarce across the country, and transportation was even worse to find since there were no gasoline supplies available. My dad drove a tractor and trailer into the city and bought approximately one hundred bags of rice (one hundred pounds each) to last what we thought would be a quick overrun of the capital city by the rebels and thereby end the fighting and war. We hid the food in a special storage room and rearranged the room so that if rebels asked us to open it, they would not know there was a hidden door. Once a week or every other, he would get us boys to load plastic ten- to fifteen-gallon rubber containers up with rice, and take food to teachers and faculty as if we were making fresh water runs. In these containers, water and rice behaved absolutely the same. Since we made similar actual water runs everyday, rebels and those people that threatened to expose us could not tell the difference. We ran this for a while and kept hundreds of people fed.

The Economic Community of West African States (ECOWAS) had combined military forces from several nations and joined the battle by sea through the shipping port of Monrovia. Their intention was to push the Taylor rebels as far from the capital as possible so as to break the constriction in order to conduct a safe cease-fire. Taylor had already been launching missiles into the city from our area. Our home had been hit with raids from military jets twice because it was attached to the administrative building of the school. Bad reconnaissance information from prior flyovers and other sources said the building was a headquarters for Charles Taylor, the rebel leader. Both raids could have been deadly since there were always some, if not all of us, present and in the home during the air strikes. But God protected us. There were others killed at home no less than three hundred yards from us on one occasion, however. There was no reason why our home shouldn't have been a similar or worse story except for God's protection. I watched the second raid on my home from a bunker knowing that my mom and dad were in the home. I lost my mind and ran out sprinting across an open area with jets still present. It was a wrong decision, to say the least, making me an easy target. I was convinced my parents were dead. I ran into our home, which was engulfed with smoke, and found my dad nestled in the intersection of two walls that provided structural safety. He informed me he had pushed my mother out of the house to safety and sent me out to find her. My mother had hidden herself in some bushes out of sight from aerial view. However, amazingly I could not find an entrance, and she could not tell me how she got in there. It did not matter; God had saved them from direct attack. That was now twice our home had been bombed with them inside.

The ECOWAS forces had really begun to step up the pressure with frequent mortar launches that were too close for comfort. We were somewhat contemplating leaving or hiding until the area was safely taken over by what we suspected was the safer occupying force. But the rebels in their haste to loot our home made that decision for us. One early morning, they came and rounded us up out of the home and told us to leave and not look back. We were kicked out of our home with AK-47 rifles at our backs and nothing but our hands in the air. In the process of raiding our home and the building in general, they found what little was left of the rice we were distributing. They found our food that we had protected to stay alive and now our lives were on the line because they were angry. According to them, my dad did not support their movement and was a traitor.

I mentioned earlier that my dad was an avid hunter and spent many days in the bushes around the campus. As a result, he was well known and liked in the local villages. When we were kicked out of our home with nowhere to go, one of those villages took us in, gave us a couple of huts to sleep in, and shared what little food they had with us. Unbeknownst to us, there was a manhunt on for us, specifically my dad, by a couple of rebel commanders. We were sitting in a hut a day or two later when a couple of rebel trucks rolled into the village with a fellow refugee that we had fed for while. He was the one that apparently told the rebels of the secret door. They gathered our family together, pushing my dad around a bit and making sure we knew they were upset. We tried to plead that it was our food, so why were they so mad? That only aggravated the situation. They ordered my sisters, my father, and a couple of adopted kids, my brother, Oscar, and I into the truck. The commander then took my youngest brother (about twelve years old), handed him to my mother, and said, "You can have this one. The rest of them we are going to kill because you and your husband lied to us." Can you imagine my mother's hurt and pain, and the helplessness she had to endure at that moment?

The head rebel in this group was a guy who was present when the commander had been threatening to shoot out my knees if I didn't fight with him. He was also a phenomenal soccer athlete as well, and he was dubbed a Brazilian nickname for his skill. I began to plead with him the whole way telling him that just like everybody else, we were simply trying to protect our lives. So how can we be wrong? About three miles into the drive he finally gave in and ordered the trucks to stop to let us out. But they decided they were still going to take and execute my dad. They also took my adopted sister, Esther, because he claimed the commander wanted her for his wife. Esther was held against her will for over a year. By the time she returned home, I had departed Liberia for the United States. It was not until I returned seventeen years later to Liberia for the first time in 2008 that I saw her again.

As for my dad, he was held in a holding cell in jail for a couple of days waiting to be executed. As far as we knew, noting the records of the rebel forces, he was dead. As a matter of fact, other rebels who considered themselves friendly came by our huts and told us he had been executed. These are the details of what happened to my dad.

He was held in the jail for two days without execution because there was an argument amongst them as to why they were going to kill him. That is very uncommon. The rebels finally decided it was time to execute him. They took him to the edge of a hill where they carried out executions. He said as he looked down he saw many bodies below. To execute a person, they stood him or her at the edge of the hill, shot him, and he fell into the pit below. He said he remembers looking down at the bodies and thinking, "Lord, all of those bodies were Your children as I am. So, if this is Your will I am ready." And he was ready to die in peace. They told him to wait at the edge so that they could go and get the blindfold. That was a ploy. They had someone hiding in the bushes that victims could not see. As they turned and walked off, the hidden person would shoot the victim and he or she would fall into the pit. This time with my dad however, the shooter unexplainably could not get the job done. They came back and got my dad after a while and put him back in the holding cell. Later in the evening, he overheard a voice speaking and asking the guard of the jail if the grey haired old man was still in the cell. The rebel went on to explain that he tried to execute him today, but something came over him. He couldn't pull the trigger. You see, the rebels were frequently into black magic and other traditional witchcraft to guard them during battle. There were even reports of cannibalism. They believed eating the heart of their enemies allowed them to invoke his strength. The more you ate, the better you would be in battle. What this shooter felt was a supernatural power indeed, but it wasn't his witchcraft. It was my God.

Through all of this overheard discussion, my dad began to realize what had just happened, and he kept praising God for giving him his life back. The next day following additional arguments between commanders over my dad's execution, one commander asked, "At this time when it is difficult even for us to find food, you are going to kill this man for trying to protect food to stay alive?" At that, they decided to take him back to the campus and set him free.

So many other incidents occurred with me and other members of my family during the Liberian civil war. I cannot tell you how it was physically possible for every one of us to go through the war and live much less remain unhurt for that matter. However, I know how it was spiritually possible—my God. Even through the many days on the run, my parents led us through devotional and prayer times. In addition to the time we had in prayer and worship as a family, my dad in recent years expressed the many times he felt the pressure on him for his family. Many times he would seek out a quiet place just to cry and ask God "Why us?" Why was his family in this place of unrest and unpredictability? There were many personal discussions with God. More importantly, we found out that God, Jehovah, is ever-present, especially in very perilous situations. God does His best work in us in the midst of such hopeless situations. It is in those times that He formulates His greatest art from the moldable clay that we are if we allow Him. But He is also an exceptional blacksmith and is great at heating up and pounding the iron we are into the shape He desires no matter how we resist His guidance. But don't just believe me if you find it difficult to do so. Listen to what the apostle Paul said the Lord told him in 2 Corinthians 12:9:

> "But he said to me, 'My grace is sufficient for you, for my power is made perfect in weakness.' Therefore I will boast all the more gladly about my weaknesses, so that Christ's power may rest on me."

I want to ask you a question, what do you think was God's purpose for me in all of the hardship and trials through war? What do you think God is seeking to accomplish with the difficult time of life He has you and/or your family? Do you think it has anything to do with Him wanting to show you through a spiritual maturation process that He is all-sufficient? I certainly think so. You know the one unique thing I learned from this time in my life? I have seen God allow every material thing I own and cherish, as well as my family's possessions (money, clothing, pictures and memoirs, home, and so on) to be taken away. I have also felt the fear that He might be taking my life or that of a loved one as well. Those situations can no longer intimidate me. More importantly, I have seen Him restore the possessions and more because of my surrender to Him, affirming His all-sufficiency. As a result, there is very little fear in me, which may be unlike you, of what happens to me if God decides to strip me of my possessions. I know the hurt of the reality, should that happen again, is inescapable. But I am miles ahead in the maturation process to absolutely realize that God can restore it all and more if He chooses as is evidenced by where I find myself today despite the hurt and destruction this chapter and book chronicles. He is now using me to express His all-sufficiency to you through this book because I surrendered to Him years ago. However take note of this fact: He didn't give me an instant platform to proclaim His formidable mercies and grace. Many times we prematurely think because we have gone through a difficult situation with God that we should receive His instant blessing of a pulpit or equivalent value. The fact that it has taken me twenty years to even consider writing about His preparation is proof that His teaching was and is no doubt ongoing. Many of God's great prophets (Moses, David, Abraham, Paul, and others) needed years of preparation for the task He had in store, as many as forty years or more in some cases. His timing is always best. Are you prepared to endure this hardship or the unfair life you feel God has dealt you in order to be molded for His use?

"Consider it pure joy, my brothers, whenever you face trials of many kinds, because you know that the testing of your faith develops perseverance. Perseverance must finish its work so that you may be mature and complete, not lacking anything" (James 1:2-4).

As if God did not want me to forget a single detail of His instruction or mistake His "all–sufficiency," He literally took me out of the midst of the war and fighting in Liberia to Coeur d'Alene, Idaho. He gave me a miraculous basketball scholarship to begin to exercise the duties He has instilled in me as the firstborn son. Fresh out of war, and with the close proximity of the Fairchild Air force base (Spokane, WA) to my home city of Coeur d'Alene, I honestly remember how frequently I would flinch and duck out of fear when I heard a military jet. You see, the sounds I experienced of fighter jets flying overhead just in passing were so distinctive for me in comparison to commercial jets; it would cause me to react to take cover. As you would recall from earlier in the chapter, I spoke of my home being bombed by jets a few times in addition to many reconnaissance missions they flew over us.

That moment of arriving in Coeur d'Alene with strong instructions on my duty from my father mentally imprinted began a journey where my training as his firstborn son expected to carry on his legacy must show its worth.

CHAPTER FOUR:

Is It a Curse, Gift, Calling/Purpose, or Passion (Motivate, Mentor, My Son...)

You ask, "What drives you to write a book about the subject of the firstborn son?" I have now lived on this earth as a firstborn son for over thirty-eight years. At various stages of my existence I have called being a firstborn son everything from a curse, a gift, a calling or purpose for my life, and a passion that I have been given by God. More importantly, this is a subject matter for which there is not a lot of information provided. As I searched the major book dealers, I was severely hard pressed to find any books or authors that targeted this subject matter, the firstborn son.

It is hard enough to live the life of a godly man in this society and even harder to live a life of a son that honors his God's, father's, parents', or elders' instructions as described in Proverbs 2:1-6:

> "My son, if you accept my words and store up my commands within you, turning your ear to wisdom and applying your heart to understanding, and if you call out for insight and cry aloud for understanding, and if you look for it as for silver and search for it as for hidden treasure, then you will understand the fear of the LORD and find the knowledge of God. For the LORD gives wisdom, and from his mouth come knowledge and understanding."

There are great mountains of responsibilities and expectations that come with the title of firstborn son or first son. Many of us first sons bear the likeness of our fathers, and as such are given the names Junior, II, III, and so on. We are no doubt, of all the kids born, expected to carry on the legacy and history of our families. Other siblings may have the luxury of committing various acts of disapprovals against the family, even as far as changing their names, but not a firstborn son. Firstborn son, there is absolutely no option for failure as the bearer of the family name. Expectations of excelling and delivering on tasks are held at a much higher standard.

On the flip side, a successful execution of duties and responsibilities by a firstborn son is as precious as gold or like a sweet melody to a family, especially his father. Since I was a little boy, I have enjoyed sounds of praises from my father in those moments when he is most proud. My father's jovial names for me come more often and so does his pet slaps, bumps of affection, and beaming smiles.

As I began to write this book, I thought it would be wise to ask my mother and father to describe any proud moments they could recall from the past. Each of them decided to give me two moments. Here is what they said in direct relay:

Mother, a bit more emotional as always, spoke of the day she gave birth to me. She has always called me "her special child" because she came very, very close to losing me at birth. Think of Africa back in the very early 1970s. The setting and conditions of hospitals at that time left much to be desired, much less the qualified training of midwives. My parents were fortunate to have access to an incredible private hospital with a great reputation throughout the West African region. My mother was brought to the hospital with ample time prior to my delivery. As such, my father departed to attend to a few other matters. In his absence she went into labor pains, ready for the delivery. There was a midwife (simply to assist the doctor) who was notorious for being insensitive with her patients and had on her record the loss of a baby already. My mother picked the short straw that day. My mother informed the midwife that she thought she was really close to delivery and asked her to please summon the doctor from his office. However, the midwife, bent on showing she knew more, did not listen to the request but instead left the room to attend to other affairs and did not notify the doctor. My mother described how she frantically hit her room's nursing station button repeatedly calling for help and no one came.

Well, a janitor passing by realized the severity of the situation and screamed for help, but my mother was deep into the process and in essence give birth to me: a stillborn. Obviously, the struggle to revive me was frantic as other nurses, aggravated by the negligence of the assigned midwife, reprimanded the woman quite heavily. It took them approximately five minutes of struggling to revive me. Not until a midwife in desperation violently shook me upside down (holding me by the legs) did I finally let out a breath and eventual cry. As a result of that incident, there were fears of brain damage and other complications to occur for me in the future. My mother describes that it is from that incident that she knew I was determined to come into this world to stay and make a mark. By God's provisions, the only sign of harm my parents noticed was severe red eyes during the first few years of life. Even that miraculously seemed to clear up as I received treatment for a severe case of pink eye (conjunctivitis) at the age of three or four. My mother has always been proud of how God brought me through to this day.

There is also a more recent event that adds fulfilling joy to her heart she says. My parents have now spent about six plus years in America. She has spent all of that time except for two to three months in my home. They came to the United States because of my father's severe cardiac illness initially suffered in Africa. As a result, they came seeking treatment. He was treated, has been in recovery, and under the supervision and observation of his cardiologist who asked for five years of monitoring to be sure my dad has no lingering effects. My siblings have not been in the position to consistently lend a helping hand to the burdens of this task.

My father came to the United States for treatment without any records of being a resident. As such, the medical burdens (financial and emotional) of covering a two-month hospital stay (practically all in ICU), rehabilitation process, as well as a new life of multiple daily medicines fell on my wife and I. They did not have medical insurance nor have they worked in the United States to be able to take advantage of social security benefits. Therefore, almost of this has been cash outlay for our family throughout this time. My mother lives in my home and has seen the times of struggle come and go over the years. She expressed how proud she is that I have not complained to my siblings or displayed any signs of animosity about the situation. She has seen me swallow the pain and keep moving forward she says.

As for my father's recollection of proud moments, he is a bit more diplomatic and astute as I have always known him to be. He says his proudest moments in recent days come frequently as he walks the halls of our church. He said his proudest moments come whenever he encounters someone who has just found out or knows he is my father. My fellow parishioners always have very nice things to say and are genuinely excited to learn that he is my father. He regularly receives praise for raising such a wonderful son, he says. My younger brother (the youngest child of the family) attends the church with his family also and is well known and liked. My dad is thrilled that his children are all living wonderful family lives and are involved with the church, the body of Christ.

What he remembers next about a proud moment, as my father goes back a few years, involves my decision to marry my wife. My father said he remembers the letter that I wrote to him and my mother (then living in Cameroon, Central Africa) to inform them of the women that I met and was considering marrying. He is extremely pleased with how I took the time to write and describe the situation that involved my love for a Caucasian woman and my desire to fully introduce her to them. I also addressed the concerns that could ensue with the blending of our cultures (African and American) and the fears of my mother that she won't be allowed to see her grandchildren. These were legitimate concerns that they had seen in the past with similar cross-cultural marriages.

I also sought to speak with them on the phone when my wife-to-be was visiting. I would frequently have my initial conversation with my family (parents and brothers), then hand the phone over to her to have a conversation with them. I would walk away and leave her to battle language barriers out on her own and develop her personal relationships. I didn't want her living vicariously through me. Such relationships needed true authenticity. She would spend most of the time talking to my brothers, but the gesture achieved its desired purpose. My father is proud about how much honor and significance I brought to them by seeking their approval although I lived thousands of miles away and could have made every excuse not to do that.

Is It a Curse?

A curse is defined as "a prayer or invocation for harm or injury to come upon one" or "a cause of great harm or misfortune."[7] This is intended to be a witty comparison, but sometimes the position of firstborn son within a family can really seem as if it is a curse. It sometimes feels as if someone did heap a prayer of misfortune upon you. You feel the need to please everyone; it seems you can do nothing right, and the measures by which you have to live seem absolutely unfair. By the way, you have inherently agreed to accept blame for everyone's mistake, and you have to fix them, too. Sound familiar...?

In an effort to teach me the characteristic of my role as the firstborn son that involves the responsibility of protecting every member of the family, my parents began that instruction quite early on in my life. I am a firstborn son who has two younger brothers and three older sisters, two of which are adopted sisters. If I chose to physically fight my younger brothers and beat on them, even if the fight was their fault, my parents expected me to handle the situation better. I would eventually pay the price for making such a poor decision. Likewise, if I got into a fight with my sisters, I should have known better that boys are not allowed to fight girls, and I subsequently had to pay the price there as well. This was a lesson and instruction to help me understand my role as the caretaker of all who are part of this family.

I remember a fight that I got into with my adopted sister who was a couple of years older than me. I was about ten at the time. My mother took us into the bedroom and proceeded to say, "So you want to fight your sister? Here's your chance." With just the three of us in the room, she began the psychological game and really roughed me up taking my shirt off before I even got to the fight. By the time I got to the fight, I had huge alligator tears rolling down my face already. Absolutely not fair I thought, no doubt. However, the lesson was learned because that was the last time I ever considered fighting a sister of mine.

All along those preteen and teenage years I continued to develop my understanding of myself with regards to confrontation, especially with family members. I remember my mother teaching me to utilize a simple breathing technique to control my temper and anger. It was as simple as counting to ten and taking deep breaths to subdue my anger whenever I felt rage coming on. As simple as it sounds, that still keeps me out of many unwanted situations.

The feeling of a curse or an unfair expectation also seemed apparent in the academic realm of our home. All of the kids in our home were practically good students; that was simply an expectation in a home of educators. However, for the firstborn son, there had to be a different mental approach toward the desire for academic success, which I briefly mentioned in chapter 2. It was not an attitude or mindset of "never fail" or "don't lose," rather it was one of understanding my responsibilities and meeting or exceeding my potential. The bar was set higher for me, and there were surely greater consequences for the slightest sign of negligence on my part. Without seeing similar demands being put on my siblings, that surely left me feeling mistreated.

Regardless of some extremely helpful tools learned, I have a confession to make. In dealing with what sometimes seemed an unfair advantage or irrational demands for handling confrontation as a young man, I carried what appeared to be a form of long-term suppressed anger. As I watched the processes of my training and nurturing unfold through my childhood, I honestly asked myself countless times if I was switched at birth, or an unwanted adoptee. It just wasn't fair. I asked myself why I wasn't allowed to react as I wanted to, especially in my defense. It had to be a curse!

Is It a Gift?

A gift is defined as "a notable capacity, talent, or endowment" or "something voluntarily transferred by one person to another without compensation."[8] The position of the firstborn son comes with many an opportunity of being called on in tough times. The decision to accept the role in its entirety within the family and pursue it with diligence and commitment does not go unnoticed.

I vividly remember my father's decision to officially bestow upon me the gift of the responsibility for the family. I had seen glimpses of his plan to do so at spots during the Liberian civil war. There were times that I was counted on to find food for the family with the help of other teenage boys that became part of the home because of homelessness. In the midst of bloodthirsty rebel soldiers, it was my responsibility to make safe decisions, and he was confident that he had trained me well. However, the actual moment of bestowal occurred on December 28, 1991, beginning at about nine or ten at night and ending about three in the morning. The next day I was boarding an airplane on my own for the first time. I was leaving the rest of my family in the midst of a civil war and would not see them for the next eight years. I would not be able to speak to them but for once a year during Christmas, and I had no idea, one day to the next, if I would receive a message that they were injured or dead.

I was handed a precious gift at the ripe and ready age of twenty. My father asked me to accept the responsibility of assuming the leadership role within the family. More importantly, he stressed that my actions in the next few years would determine the fate of my family. It was great to hear those words as they put me on a mission. It is extremely hard to put into words, how I felt that day, but I still cherish it to this day. I was committed to the gift, pursued it, and no doubt, the rest of the family has embraced and acknowledged it. It is an awesome feeling. It is an awesome gift. But take heed; even gifts have the ability to destroy. In other words, that awesome gift of responsibility I received from my father and family was the one that drove the extremely strong bond I possess. Due to my mismanagement, I came extremely close to ruining my marriage and would have subsequently robbed myself of the incredible immediate family the Lord has blessed me with. That gift almost robbed me of the birth of my precious firstborn son Garrison, whose life motivates me to write this book.

Is It My Calling and My Life's Purpose?

A purpose is defined as "something set up as an object or end to be attained" or "a subject under discussion or an action in course of execution."[9] There are times that I assess situations that I find myself in and wonder how I navigate or manage to maintain my composure and focus concerning the task at hand. I am by no stretch of the imagination a perfect or flawless person. Thank goodness Jesus Christ has set the bar out of reach for a fallen soul like me, and God emphatically stamps it in Scripture by stating "all have sinned and fall short of the glory of God" (Rom. 3:23). I have just sensed all my life that there is a mission, purpose, or a goal to attain, especially as one others rely on. Therefore, I cannot afford to spend time being consumed by distractions. My wife frequently accuses me of having the ability to cut things out of my life instantly that would normally take others weeks and months to do. I seem fortunate to avoid developing an addictive personality to any thing or any person, besides the family that God has entrusted to me. I seem to understand or sense when calm is in order rather than aggressiveness or retaliation. If I find that something in my life is destructive and has to go, then it is time to make a decision and remove it. Purposeful living has truly become second nature and an extraordinary fact of my life. After a lengthy existence in such a role, I certainly realize it is a calling on my life much like the career choice of a pastor or a life's calling of work in the body of Christ.

When it comes to purposeful living as it pertains to the life of the firstborn son and his upbringing or development, a common and frequent pitfall is the area of friendships. What choice of friends do we select, and who truly assumes the leadership role or allows himself to be influenced or persuaded regularly? You see, I am blessed with many seemingly lifelong friends. From my childhood days on into these middle years, I can't remember many people that I have deliberately chosen to refuse to be friends with. They are all my friends to this day. However, I believe one of the greatest attributes that lends to that blessing is the fact that I am not a follower. Nor do I approach my friends or interact with them claiming or seeking to be a leader. Nevertheless, I frequently find myself in positions of leadership predominantly via the request of others. That calling on my life that expects people to rely on me soon assumes responsibility for my surroundings. There seems to be an unintimidating aura and integrity about me that seems to remove the feeling of a threat that my friends may feel. But don't mistake that for not being direct and truthful.

I have been blessed with the ability to draw friendships that contain significant substance. For instance, it is not uncommon for me to receive multiple calls and text messages each day from friends who have seriously impactful life questions. These are questions affecting their lives and their families for which they trust my judgment and confidentiality. No, I am not a psychologist or any sort of guru. There is just no question in my friends' minds I will do my best to give them my committed, honest, and scripturally-based advice.

Speaking of following, or being persuaded, versus leading, I remember a college situation that involved a major brawl at the dormitory because a racist comment was made to an African-American teammate. My teammate came to the verbal defense of a friend who was being physically pushed around by another student. Both of them in the initial confrontation were Caucasian males. However, a bit intoxicated, the young man doing the pushing sadly chose racial slurs as his primary verbal communication tool. Before long, there was an all-out brawl and desire to hurt the fellow that made the statement by approximately ten African-American males. The dormitory director, resident advisors, and myself fought to barricade doors preventing a larger crowd from gathering and generating a riot. It took close to ten police cars and officers surrounding the dormitory to calm that situation down. That incident ended up with expulsions and suspensions of several people from the college. Regardless of my skin color and the comment that was made, I found myself fighting to maintain tempers of teammates raging in severe anger rather than letting my youthful testosterone reign. I could identify with their angers. The environment on the campus was extremely sensitive to racism. As divisive a statement as that was, I had been taught how to restrain my emotions and avoid the trance and swells of the crowd. I am not a follower.

Emotional control is very vital to the nature of the firstborn son and is a huge compliment to his leadership quality. I truly attribute my understanding of this nature and component of my personality to the upbringing my dad instilled when it came to discipline. He really demanded responsible and matured thinking from each of us quite early. All of my siblings seem to possess similar subdued responses to challenging incidents rather than being reactive. So it must be his doing. My dad was not a big fan of spanking as a disciplinary action, but when he did spank, we knew he was dishing out something fierce. When we disobeyed, he asked us to imagine each of us had a long rope that connected us to him. Depending on how severe an incident it was, we just cut a piece of that rope which subsequently got us closer to him. The incident that "cut the last piece" and consumed the rope got us up close and personal with him was the one that initiated a spanking. His wish was that his children, as he described it, "would shoulder their own problems." In other words, he was not going to utilize spanking on every incident to cultivate mature thinking and behavior in his kids. He expected us to use a matured behavior and thought process when faced with a situation rather than fear as a motivator. That really taught us to take responsibility for our actions. He always noted to us and to his students, as dean of discipline, that beating and spanking is for horses because it makes them run harder. He expected us to examine our actions and resolve the issue, or make sure it didn't happen again if our actions could not be corrected. I believe that thoughtful approach caused us each to avoid reactive behaviors. I cannot hesitate to note as Scripture says in Proverbs 13:24, "spare the rod and spoil the child," that at some level fear of my dad's spanking was enough to make us pursue maturity at an early age.

In an attempt to assure maturity was an early ingredient of my development as a firstborn son, my father truly did not spare the rod, even in the teenage years. My final spanking came as a result of a grave disobedience to direct instructions from my father. It was his final words to me following the disciplinary action that are the most memorable to this day. I will mention those words at the end of telling this story. I informed my father of my intentions to make a vegetable garden. I informed him of my plans to burn and set fire to an area behind our home to do so. It was the dry season in Liberia, which meant six months of equatorial sunshine and daily weather highs of over one hundred degrees Fahrenheit. During this time of the year, the grass is absolutely brown and scorched by the sunrays. My father instructed me not to start a fire but instead utilize a grass cutter for my project. He then drove into the city for a very important diplomatic meeting.

When my father returned, all he saw as far as his eyes could see was black burnt ground. I am sure you can tell by now what happened. I nearly burned down the campus, and it required at least forty persons including machinery to get the fire under control. I received a severe spanking for my actions. I think it took just one cut to consume my long rope that day. This was the summer prior to beginning my freshmen year in high school. My father's final words were, "This is the last time I am ever going to spank you. If you continue to make decisions that are this disappointing, it is unfortunate, but you will have to live your life with the consequences." In other words, it was up to me to now take significant ownership of my maturation since my recent action proved incredibly disappointing. Otherwise, the would-be pain of my ongoing errors, though costly to my family and me as the firstborn son, would have to be my teacher. I don't believe there has been another incident that was as costly or required such an exchange with my father.

Consider this: When it comes to purposeful living and a calling such as that of a firstborn son, only God preordains our path long before our birth. The Lord took me through an upbringing that was greatly uncommon by African standards. It was truly uncommon to be raised in an environment of learning with high international diversity and with a great many modern amenities.

The Lord then took me through a civil war that incredibly tested my fortitude and my willingness to stand up to individuals and situations that threatened my life. At that age and era of my life, such a stance was unpopular when it came to my survival and some of my peer relationships. The Lord makes my next stops Coeur d'Alene, Idaho, and Butte, Montana. If you know the history and reality of racism in each of these locations at the moments in time I happened to live in these cities, there is great humor that God would see fit to foster critical points of my maturation there. Yet, nothing speaks more powerfully of God's ordination on my life, as well as His wisdom in preparing me, than a hindsight view of the path He chose. God uses the foolish things in the world's, yours, and my eyes to put our wisdom to shame.

Coeur d'Alene was a place that was heavily influenced by racism. I had a great NIC (North Idaho College) family that embraced, loved, and provided me with an unforgettable experience during my time there. However, with Hayden Lake the home of the KKK (Ku Klux Klan) not far north of Coeur d'Alene, there frequently occurred what I would call racist drive-bys. Usually at night, when there was not clear visibility to the faces behind the comments, elements of that group would drive by, turn their headlamps off, slow down enough to scream a racist comment, and speed away so that I couldn't see the license plate. I also remember an ex-girlfriend's new boyfriend calling my house and screaming racist comments through the phone from miles away, and I had no idea where he lived. I offered to have us meet so he could express his sentiment genuinely and in person, but he chose to not call again.

As I made a decision to head out to continue my education in Montana, many of my workmates, who were older men, asked why I chose a tough and racist place like Butte, Montana. By the way, I lived in Coeur d'Alene at the time. Is that humorous or what? I answered, "The same reason I chose a place like Coeur d'Alene—God prepared it." Nevertheless, nothing and no one could have prepared me for this next stage in my experience but God.

In Butte, I spent a lot of time as an athlete speaking to kids at elementary and high schools, as well as earning the general trust of families and university staff as a role model within the community. I had resided in the town for two years by now, made the newspaper frequently as an athlete, and was well known and liked around town. My roommate, Ryan Alston, and I came into the school and community together knowing what we were walking into and committed with a purpose to defuse all stereotypes. Ryan was an African-American teammate from the south side of Chicago, Illinois. We were teammates at NIC in Coeur d'Alene and decided to attend Montana Tech together. We committed to each other to excel in academics, athletics, and incredibly defeat all stereotyped expectations of what African-American young men were in the minds of many in this community.

We also had an awesome local family (Rodney and Marylee James) that literally embraced and loved us but truly made our stay in Montana absolutely unforgettable. Rod was a highly-esteemed professor and dean at the college we attended. We were loved and attended to as they would their own children. Rod would sit with us and talk through difficult games performances when we needed the lift; he would take us on hunting or fishing trips or teach us to ride horses just like a father would. They attended every single game we played at home or away it seemed. They took us to their home for meals and more. Marylee fed us well every weekend and made sure we were comfortable enough as we slept through Sunday NFL football games in her bean bags (a college kid's joy) and on couches. We shared stories and laughter with their children who were mine and Ryan's ages and older. Marylee, an incredible mother, always knew what sons would forever love and cherish. She gave us each a large album full of newspaper clippings about us of our senior year of athletics and other important moments. A master embroider, she also gave us amazing memory quilts of our lives. For me the quilt vividly spoke of my life in Liberia right on through my years in Montana with Rod and Marylee James and their family.

Regardless of all of the good will I received in Montana, what happened in my next occurrence I describe was hard to endure, except for a commitment to a calling and purpose for my life. Teena, now my wife, and I were dating at the time. She and a couple of her friends located a great house for rent quite close to the campus. The owner was extremely accommodating and went as far as offering to furnish the house and more since he had found an impressive group of young ladies to rent his property. The agreement was completed, and it was time to move in. I went to help my girlfriend with the move and had just taken a load of things into the house. I came out for more things and could not find Teena anywhere.

I began to walk down the block looking for her, and as I looked into the window of the home next door, I saw her silhouette with an adult male in a confrontational posture standing before her. As I began to rush toward the door to make sense of what I was seeing, she came rushing out and asked that we please leave immediately. It was the owner, and he had seen me entering the house with things. He called her over and approached her in aggravation stating, "No nigger was welcomed on his property or allowed in his house." She informed him that we were dating and as such she (and friends) would not be renting his home noting his racist preference. It took a lot to avoid retaliating in a much more aggressive manner, but I was able to walk away calmly. God had prepared me to handle and face difficult situations long before. Furthermore, the consequences that awaited me for a compromising reaction as a firstborn son would have been far more costly than the temporary satisfaction.

So, Why Write This Book About the Firstborn Son?

So we go back to the original question, "What drives me to write a book about the subject of the firstborn son?" The word *passion* is defined as "suffering" or "the state or capacity of being acted on by external agents and forces" or "intense, driving, or overmastering feeling or conviction."[10] I find it difficult to claim any of the attributes discussed earlier (curse, gift, or purpose) as the single defining attribute of a firstborn son.

The range of emotions from situations of difficulty on through to the thrilling moments of joy I have experienced forces me to label the mental approach and strongest attribute of a first-born son as *passion*. I no longer despise the hard decisions necessary to fulfill my role. I stay even-keeled in embracing the gifts and purposeful existence I have been afforded as well. However, it is the end results of each situation I am faced with that generates an overwhelming conviction and acceptance of my role. It is a passion.

I write this book because I have the passion to motivate my family that has embraced me as the firstborn son. I write because I have the passion to motivate my friends and others that choose to read and seek to shape their mentality around difficult responsibilities. I write this book to remind me of the responsibility I have to my firstborn son to teach him the meaning and importance of his role. I write this book because our society is morally paralyzed by the lack of young men who understand the sacrificial role required of them within the family structure. The family is the foundational component of society. Our society reflects what comes out of our homes, or should I say, what we send out of our homes as parents, but more so as fathers.

It is the predictions of Scripture written over a thousand years ago that has so vividly described the nature of men walking our streets today as so-called fathers and knights-in-shining-armor of their wives. Let's not forget the collection of single men out there who fancy themselves as desirable marriage materials for our daughters and sisters. Men, too often we live our lives selfishly focused on ourselves rather than the responsibilities (our dependents and righteous duties and tasks) the Lord has called us to. We have bought the worldly lie that the life we live is about *us* rather than a sacrificial outpour of ourselves for others. We continue to raise our sons and the future leaders of our nations to perpetuate the same selfish disease we possess, but it seems to exponentially increase from one generation to the next. This is what the Scripture I referenced earlier says:

> "But mark this: There will be terrible times in the last days. People will be lovers of themselves, lovers of money, boastful, proud, abusive, disobedient to their parents, ungrateful, unholy, without love, unforgiving, slanderous, without self-control, brutal, not lovers of the good, treacherous, rash, conceited, lovers of pleasure rather than

lovers of God— having a form of godliness but denying its power. Have nothing to do with them" (2 Tim. 3:1-5).

Men is this not incredible how spot on this Scripture is in attestation to the lives society applauds us for living. We pursue our careers, toys, hobbies, wealth, relationships, and even our trophy wives in all design to provide self-satisfaction and proof of "lovers of themselves." We are being encouraged and enticed to love ourselves by intoxicating commercials, billboards, Internet, movies, magazines, music, bad theology and doctrine (*form of godliness but denying its power*), the lure of prosperity and so on.

All through this book, I will motivate you through humorous and challenging real life stories. You have experienced a bit of those already. I will motivate sons, those that want to motivate their sons and daughters, and particularly firstborn sons to step up and take the reins on the amazing horsepower in the life they possess. If we submit our lives in obedience as available to be used in the proper godly context, we render ourselves available for "every" (not some) good work. Disobedience, on the other hand, results in the generational degradation described in Scripture as "*evildoers and impostors will go from bad to worse, deceiving and being deceived*" (2 Tim. 3:13, italics mine).

I write this book because of my desire to mentor others coming after me. I have spent several years as a youth athletic coach and have been blessed with some wonderful friendships and relationships. The youth and adults have taught me some amazing lessons. My vow to them is that I will live a life that will not bring shame to them. Especially for the youth, I will live an exemplary life that will allow them to consistently have a source of mentoring. It is amazing to hear a young man say, "I thank you for being the consistent male figure in my life even in the tough times."

I have walked a good portion of my life's journey in this role. Many men out there can claim they have walked in this role all their life as well. However, how many men have walked this road in full awareness and embrace of their responsibilities as dictated by the role of the firstborn son? I expect a much longer way to go in this life as a father and firstborn son if God allows me His longevity. I write this book to stand up as mentor to those in need.

I write this book for my firstborn son. Just yesterday, August 30, 2009, Garrison Asher Bambolo was dedicated (not baptized) to the Lord by our family at church. During the ceremony, as parents we make a vow to raise our son in the way of the Lord. As a father, I am required to be the kind of godly man, not simply a Christian, that my son seeks to emulate.

Many of us want a Christian acquaintance for a friend, spouse, or relative as opposed to someone who has committed to being godly. There is a difference. The Holy Bible demands that we are godly; we absolutely seek to be like Jesus Christ in attitude and behavior. Vine's Expository Dictionary of New Testament Words uses the Greek word *eusebos* for *godly* to describe this requirement which is "to live (of manner of life)."[11] In 2 Timothy 3, Paul describes clearly what ungodliness in Christians will look like in the last days, the era we now live in. Read the chapter, then look around you attentively and see if that description does not fit many of the churches and Christians you know. However in the same chapter, he describes for young Timothy what godly living is by describing what Timothy saw as godly living in Paul's and others' lives. Paul then goes on to climax the chapter with a famous verse many of us have recited frequently. However we fail to grab hold of the critical instruction of this verse. If I intend to train my son Garrison and my children in the ways of the Lord I must grasp and hold fast to this instruction.

> "All Scripture is God-breathed and is useful for teach-
> ing, rebuking, correcting and training in righteousness, so
> that the man of God may be thoroughly equipped for
> every good work" (2 Tim. 3:16-17).

Garrison is a firstborn son, and much like any other firstborn son he will have very similar challenges. There will be days that he probably feels his daddy is demanding too much of him. There will be days he will probably feel he is cursed, gifted, or purpose-filled. Most of all, it is my prayer he will find that it is his God-ordained passion to become a Proverbs 2 son that drives him.

Finally, I write this book simply because as surprising as this may sound, there are seemingly no books on this subject matter.

There are no books written with the intent of guiding, more importantly training, a young man on the realistic challenges of being a firstborn son. It would be one thing if I didn't find enough bestsellers on the subject matter. However, I am shocked to notice that the major retailers had no bestsellers, nor did they have *any* sellers it appeared. Our society continues to propagate the feminizing of young men who no longer want to embrace their roles as their father's sons. As a matter of fact, what matters anymore is what selfishly pleases them. Ultimately, this helps to contribute to higher divorce rates and fatherless children since they lack the tools and skills to live selflessly and sacrificially for others rather than themselves. Honestly men, this life is not about you or me, instead it is about God.

Legacy is defined as "something transmitted by or received from an ancestor or predecessor from the past."[12] My father passed down his legacy for what he expects of a Bambolo. In a desire to honor my father, I have sought to preserve his teachings to the best of my ability. Much of the same desires now spur me on that my son, my firstborn son, Garrison, will proudly advance the legacy of the Bambolo name. I must ensure that his soul is nourished with fertile ground for the Bambolo Legacy to flourish.

For those who don't feel you have a legacy to follow, much less pass on, let this book provide you with a framework to create your legacy to pass on to your son(s). The DNA you pass along to your kids is not simply in your genes. *The life your kids see you live is the biggest architectural blueprint they have to construct their own.* However long it takes, they will revert to that DNA and structural design for life you handed them as the master architect. In other words, they will respond the way you do to adversity or joy, marital strife, anger, forgiveness, gratitude, attitude toward work, and more. I will go out on a limb to assume you love your children to an immeasurable degree and want the absolute best for them. Pause for a second and consider this next question: Are you thrilled with what you've handed them? If so or if not, let's take a closer look and refine your legacy in the chapters to come beginning with the spousal selection, keeping in mind it is for life because divorce leaves a nasty scar on **all** involved. Either way you answer the question, I have no doubt both you and I can absorb teaching from the Scriptures to leave that greater architectural design as our legacy.

"Blessed be the God and Father of our Lord Jesus Christ, the Father of sympathy (pity and mercy) and the God [Who is the Source] of every comfort (consolation and encouragement), Who comforts (consoles and encourages) us in every trouble (calamity and affliction), so that we may also be able to comfort (console and encourage) those who are in any kind of trouble or distress, with the comfort (consolation and encouragement) with which we ourselves are comforted (consoled and encouraged) by God" (2 Cor. 1:3-4, AMP).

CHAPTER FIVE:

Firstborn Son, Who Is Your Wife, and Why Did She Pick You?

I first met my lovely wife on the campus of North Idaho College in Coeur d'Alene, Idaho. No, it wasn't love at first sight and neither one of us was swept off our feet at first sight. But the journey that we have taken together, sometimes holding hands, and sometimes refusing to hold hands along the way, has proven and taught us that love at first sight could never have accomplished in this union what God has by His design.

We come from extremely different worlds. Never in a million years would I have scripted the marital union of an African boy from a small township in Liberia, West Africa, to a Caucasian American girl from and even smaller town in the middle of Idaho. We fell in love in the backyard of the KKK just outside of Hayden Lake, Idaho. Now, can you tell me that our God does not have a sense of humor? Probably not…

Why Did She Pick Me?

We met through the introduction of a mutual friend. My wife and I playfully argue to this day about who initiated the actual expression of interest and how. So I won't go into details about that at this time. But I will mention that neither one of us was pursuing Christ nearly as much as we are now. I, for sure, sadly lived a double life as a Sunday Christian. As an international student, I was allowed to work only on the campus of the school I attended. Although I had graduated from North Idaho College (NIC) a year removed and now lived and schooled in Butte, Montana, I came back to Coeur d'Alene to work that summer because the area presented more activities (work, social life, Pro-Am Basketball summer workouts, and so on.). Teena, as a collegiate volleyball athlete, came into school mid-summer to begin practices for the upcoming season. I stayed in Coeur d'Alene a few weeks longer to wrap up a part I played in the local summer theater production. We happened to live in the same apartment complex and as such were introduced.

As we spent time talking and discovering more about each other over the next few weeks we had together, I discovered a woman unlike any other I had met in my life. I found a woman who was strong, independent, intelligent, confident, honest, beautiful (internally and externally), and definitely had her life so well planned out at the age of 19. She new what she wanted to accomplish personally and professionally at any given age you would call out in the future. As an example, she wanted to be a mother by age twenty-eight. And I can attest that she stayed right on track for that and still does on other things to this day.

Teena happened to be in a relationship with someone at the time, and she would not allow me to get close to her although we both knew there was an attraction. This made it even tougher, because remember that men are built as conquerors. My desire to pursue and conquer this beauty became even stronger after she portrayed that quality. But she made me wait until she was no longer in that relationship, and I did.

Firstborn son, what qualities are you looking for in a partner, and are you willing to wait for her to be ready?

"So, why me" I asked her. When I left home in Africa, after just breaking out of the teenage years, my parents had given me a mission to accomplish. As Teena and I shared our thoughts through conversations, she began to uncover the sense of what that mission was and how critical it was for me to accomplish that mission. She understood as well that there were personal sacrifices I had resolved internally to accept as the price for accomplishing the mission. Some of those sacrifices focused on my social lifestyle and wardrobe, the saving of work-study income to send money home rather than ask for money from my parents (like the typical college student), and the choice of avoiding parties and spending Friday nights in the gym or dorm room instead.

I left my family in the midst of a treacherous civil war in Liberia during which my parents lost everything they ever worked for in life during the course of close to thirty years as missionaries. We were forced to leave our home with nothing but AK-47 rifles pointed at our backs. When we got a chance to come back to the house weeks later, it was emptied of everything. It was my duty in the USA to study hard and succeed at whatever I did as the only hope to restore the family. As a result I couldn't afford to have any distractions from my goals.

I wasn't perfect by any stretch of the imagination, but I knew my priorities. I knew where I was going and had no choice but to get there. My wife says that was the quality that attracted her to me. She was impressed that I knew what I had to accomplish, and I had a clear plan of how I was going to do so. In addition, her attraction to me was also centered on her observation of how much love I had for my family. She had never before seen such a bond between a young man at my age and his family, especially siblings. She said that is why she picked me. Little did we know that bond with my family would also cost our marriage dearly as you will see later in this chapter.

I tell you about this part of my life as an even greater testimony to my wife Teena's character. I am a poor African boy. I have no money, material things, or promises of inheritance to offer her. There is no *Coming to America* Eddie Murphy script for her. As a matter of fact, all I have to offer is baggage and burdens that come with me and require money that I don't possess. She saw all of that and even chose to utter the words, "I love you, and want to be there with you to help you accomplish that goal." Wow, does God have a plan in place for my life or what?

In the beginning of our relationship, I underestimated my wife. Many men underestimate their wives and fail to fully grasp the depth of a woman's emotional commitment when she is properly loved by her mate. A woman deeply and securely in love with her husband will unquestionably walk through fire with him if she can trust and be assured he is there for her and will be there always fulfilling his commitment to her. My wife and I have seen some tough times, but her promise to be there with me to accomplish those goals has been true. It (promise) continues to be a powerful pillar in our lives.

It was approximately eight years after I left Liberia when Teena and I married. It was about three years after I graduated from college, and Teena had also graduated a little over a year prior. We had been dating for a little over three years. We were absolutely new to our professions and not nearly generating substantial income. I hadn't seen my family in all that time, except for my sister, whom I'd seen on two occasions. A costly marriage loomed in addition to a burning desire to see the rest of my family. For two young ambitious love birds with the aspirations but certainly not the reality of making large incomes soon, the American dream catcher called the credit card was too enticing to pass up. So we made the commitment to add to an already stiff cost mounted by the wedding the cost of the dream to fly my family to the United States. Although my family had left war-ravished Liberia for the safety of Cameroon, Africa), their living conditions had not improved much. Therefore, it seemed a great opportunity and finally a chance to truly begin to fulfill the mission of family restoration bestowed upon me by my parents.

Those decisions were just the beginning of my wife's committed sacrifice. We did get my family here to the United States, and our wedding went well as an incredibly beautiful ceremony. However, after my brothers got here, it dawned on me that they were not getting any younger scholastically, but they also had some incredible musical talents as vocalists that we could take advantage of in furthering the mission of restoration. With a month or two left before their visas expired, we went into high gear securing auditions with several colleges and received some offers of substantial partial scholarships. Since they were international students, we still had a significant amount of money to secure in order to complete the requirements for receipt of the I-22 legal immigration student status to stay in the United States. To do so we had to commit to take out a sizeable amount of student loans on their behalf. So, we did that. As for my parents, they returned to Cameroon after the wedding. Nonetheless, I had practically accomplished the initial goal to at least get the family back on its feet with absolutely no shortage of support from my new bride.

I have to make this small note that an even greater statement of sacrifice, tolerance, and acceptance was made by my wife. For the hardships of the African culture this kind of sacrifice was normal. But for the luxuries of the American culture, we tackled all of these challenges and mounted these scary amounts of financial debt with my brothers living with us in our tiny two bedroom condo from day one of our wedding and life together. I cannot tell you why she didn't ask for divorce right then and there because this locomotive we were riding wasn't slowing down anytime soon.

The First Six Years...

Firstborn son, you cannot measure the importance of finding a woman of virtue. If you are not married, I encourage you to wait until you find one. If you are already married, and you don't think you have a woman of virtue, lead the woman you have to become one. Unlike what most people think, leading does not mean you *tell* her how to become a woman of virtue. Leading in this case means, you set the bar of achievement as a man of God so high that the life *you* lead is what pulls her to become a woman of virtue. Yes, it is absolutely possible, I speak from experience. If you don't know what a woman of virtue looks like, read and glean from Proverbs 31.

My wife and I came into marriage for all intents and purposes the right reasons. We were truly deep in love and had all of the deep invisible bonds that tie a couple together. We had a purpose and a cause to fight for together, sports, similar educational interests, each other and more. However, I truly never really intended to share that purpose and goal that centered on me. I felt that she would really never understand. So all through our dating years, I fought to push her away claiming I was protecting her because she really didn't understand. Unfortunately, I took that desire to push her away into our marriage approximately three and half years after we initially met. Teena, on the other hand, never failed to keep her promise.

The cultural differences between my wife and I surely existed and took over my wife overwhelmingly. I have to admit that after our wedding ceremony I set her up with a four-hour drive back to Seattle alone with my parents. (The wedding was performed in Coeur d'Alene with sentiments toward where we met as a couple, however we lived in Seattle.) During that drive she got a lot of intimate details of the load I brought into our marriage from my parents. Eventually we sat in our condo to talk with my parents before they returned to Africa. My wife is two years younger than one of my brothers and one year older than the other. In true African fashion, my father proceeds to tell her that as the wife of the firstborn son, she is now mother to these two young men, and they are obligated to obey her at all cost. As the wife of the first-born son, she also assumes a position of authority within the family that is specifically reserved. To me, this was not much different than what I heard from my dad eight years prior, and it didn't really affect me. My wife, however, was completely caught off guard about the fact that she was now expected to mother men, much less men older than and as old as her. The knowledge of her newfound authoritative role did not bring any lighter expectations as well.

Here is the point of explaining all of this. I began to make some horrible decisions upon feeling the desperation and sense of urgency that arose from the additional financial burdens and other necessities we had just taken on board.

My plate was full. I was not sharing the burden, and I felt the urge to pick up the pace on our finances and other much-needed areas of my life without really including God or my wife in the plans. With designs of building an international business, I began traveling frequently to Asia in an attempt to restore my family into full swing, among other desires. I conveniently moved my wife to about fourth or fifth on the list of my life's most important matters.

I was realizing success in my plans and dreams to restore my family that I left in the midst of civil war in Africa. I had designs of building a multi-million-dollar international business that showed some promise. God was conveniently available when I needed Him, or so I thought. Even basketball and other important social duties took precedence over messages and distracting signs that I knew all too well existed on the roadmap of ideology I was on and that I had to navigate through.

> "For this reason a man will leave his father and mother and be united to his wife, and the two will become one flesh" (Eph. 5:31).

Firstborn son, I knew all too well what that verse means. But I chose to hide behind the seemingly noble things I was doing to restore my family. I claimed that the business building was absolutely going to set us free financially, so I was shocked that my wife chose to complain rather than accept her portion of sacrifice in this marital relationship. I further justified my actions by feeling good about myself. I had never really been a drinker or party person, out for clothes and material things such as cars, nor was I a womanizer. So, when compared to most guys that I knew, I wasn't perfect, but I was doing a lot better than most. Is that really what matters my fellow firstborn sons, comparing ourselves to our buddies? If that is what we believe then we are really in sin and "missing the mark" on what our God-given role is. The real question is "How am I doing when compared to Christ?" Here is the order by which Paul tells Christians to follow:

> "PATTERN YOURSELVES after me [follow my example], as I imitate and follow Christ (the Messiah)" (1 Cor. 11:1, AMP).

Learning to Love Her as Jesus Christ Loved

The goal is to live for perfection. Remember, we may fall, but it is not time for navel gazing. Instead, we are in the best position to look up and see our Father's hand reaching out to pick us up, dust us of, and send us on to conquer ultimate success.

I titled the previous segment "the first six years" because of this. My wife has told me that it takes her six years to really come into full acceptance of a flaw of mine, a major change in our lives, or any significant request good or bad. So at year six of our relationship and her observation that I wasn't seeking to cleave to her, she became emotionally disconnected from me and subsequently thought it was time to find a new life. When a woman emotionally disconnects from her husband, only God can reestablish that connection. Not many men allow themselves to achieve true emotional and soulful connections with their wives. We frequently sabotage our attempts at achieving success without even noticing or knowing it. Many of us have bought the lies of the culture, Hollywood, and the media that misrepresents what our marital commitments should be.

I never imagined I would hear the word *divorce* from my wife's lips. She had observed some circumstances in her upbringing that clearly defined her views on marriage and divorce. So with that said, after I finally worked up the courage to propose to her, Teena informed me that divorce was not an option for her, and she was in it for life. So need I say, it took a long time and a lot of courage for her to be prepared to finally say to me, "If you want a divorce from me, you can have it." It completely caught me off guard because I never ever uttered the words "I want a divorce" to her. However, my choices and actions toward her screamed it loudly for six long years. We were in a relationship all right, but we never really connected mentally, emotionally, or spiritually.

We (especially me) had to put on the new person in Christ. Here is the verse my wife professed as the epitome of her Christian baptismal commitment. This is the verse that is the catalyst for change from the person she was to the one she is now since she has accepted Jesus Christ into her life:

> "You were taught, with regard to your former way of life, to put off your old self, which is being corrupted by its deceitful desires; to be made new in the attitude of your minds; and to put on the new self, created to be like God in true righteousness and holiness" (Eph. 4:22-24).

It was not until we put God at the forefront of our lives and relationship that we began to learn the nature of the love we needed.

The kind of love I am speaking about is best personified in Christian circles as *agape* love. This kind of love in its ultimate distinction is best described in the attitude of God's love toward His Son Jesus Christ, as well as us His children, and toward all mankind. Some Scripture verses that personify agape love are John 3:16, John 17:26, and Romans 5:8. It is love that is given or offered without just cause. In other words, there is nothing we have done that qualifies us as recipients of God's holy and omnipotent love. As a matter of fact, many of our daily actions and thoughts deserve His wrath. Yet, it is His love that He chooses to give. For me as a husband and follower of Christ, this is not love that is based of feelings, natural inclinations, or an affinity for satisfaction my wife has given me. Rather this love is based on the fact and command of God's Word if I intend to be a godly husband and personify God's nature.

My love for my wife as a friend, helper, equal partner, mother of my children, and lover will never be fulfilled if I do not understand and fully pursue the incorporation of agape love. The same goes for my wife's desire to love me and our desire to love our children. Hollywood and novels paint all kinds of wrong views of love, sexual, appearance, wealth, and so forth. In case you haven't heard it before, I am here to tell you that love is a choice, a choice that is best exercised unconditionally.

Think about this for a second, as I also did: Too many men get into romantic relationships and subsequently marriage hoping to find pleasure rather than purity. I am not saying seeking pleasure is a bad thing at all. What I do want you to consider if you haven't approached your relationship as such, is this: We should first seek and pursue purity, which consequently produces clean and healthy pleasure. Here are some definitions of *purity* out of the Webster's 1828 dictionary: "Freedom from guilt or the defilement of sin; innocence; as purity of heart or life. Chastity; freedom from contamination by illicit sexual connection."[13] Uniquely, purity is one of those words that is significantly understood across differentiating lines of Christians, non-Christians, cultures, creeds, and many more. Simply said, if the object of examination isn't pure then it is contaminated. Purity in marriage brings forth immense pleasure in so many facets (spoken and unspoken communication, decision making, family unity, sexual intimacy, and so on), and it removes all threats or intimidation. It was not until I found purity in my marriage that the pleasure of being a husband and father has skyrocketed and frequently over-whelms me with its blessings.

My good friend, Dr. Ken Hutcherson, in his marriage and relationship seminar calls marriage the closest thing to the Holy Trinity on Earth. In essence there is true equality across the par-ties of the relationship, in roles there is a much-needed positional hierarchy. There are essences and roles that reflect the pure and non-threatening relationship of the parties of the Trinity, as well as the husband and wife to help us grasp the concept fully. (See Appendix B for Scripture verses that support this.)

In likening marriage to the Trinity, the wife fills the role of the Holy Spirit, the husband fills the role of the Son, Jesus Christ (sacrificial living till death), and God the Father maintains the head role.

Firstborn son, do you love your wife as Christ loved the church? Do you love her enough to die to yourself (and see her as more important than you) for her everyday and take the abuse for her and sometimes from her? Have you thought about how often our churches abuse Christ in our failure to stand on the Bible with our actions for Him? Firstborn son, are you prepared to physically be beaten and die for your wife as Christ did for the church? Not unless you connect to your wife, in love, as Christ did for the church (His bride) will you understand the pure and sacrificial love He commands and thereby achieve a soulful and an emotional connection, that of Ephesians 5:25-33, to your wife.

My Proverbs 31 Wife

The reconnection process was not an easy one. It required me to take some drastic steps to learn the trust and love that I had to have. I started to use the word *restore* in the previous sentence, but

I can't use it because now that I know what that kind of sacrificial love is, I never had it in the first place. Do you have it, or have you had it? Think about that for a moment.

Through all of this my wife was fully prepared to move on with her life. She never expected that I would desire to fight for my marriage above all the other things that had assumed priority over her. But the roadmap had been put before me long before this occurred. I just chose the detour over the narrow road. Deep down inside, I knew divorce was not an option, especially with parents who had been married for over thirty-five years at the time. Please do not see having the roadmap or the Bible as a pat on the back for me or you. Because having it and being trained on it but not using it is too great a failure!

My wife left my home and moved in with a friend for about three or four months while we seemingly tried to make some attempts to finalize the divorce. With bitterness, pride, and desperation, I crawled into what has now become our home church and sought help knowing quite well that was my last hope. A man from there who became a great friend put himself at risk and went knocking on a corporation's door to ask for an angry woman he didn't know at all. He said to her, "You need to come and talk to our pastor about saving your marriage." Praise be to God since He is still in the business of restoration, instructing, and teaching.

> "Come to me, all you who are weary and burdened, and I will give you rest. Take my yoke upon you and learn from me, for I am gentle and humble in heart, and you will find rest for your souls. For my yoke is easy and my burden is light" (Matt. 11:28-30).

The process of learning God's kind of love required me to shed almost everything that stood in the way of our relationship in order to learn sacrificial love. Friends that did not represent the life I was choosing to lead had to go; the business had to go; my love for the game of basketball and Pro-Am tournaments had to go; even my family had to take a backseat for a good long while until I learned how to love my wife properly. As time went by, the process was not about me seeking all of the avenues by which I could train my wife to love me best. The process required me to introspectively examine myself and my relationship with Jesus Christ (how well did I know the roadmap?).

My focus and energy was directed toward my growth in Christ and taking on His yoke. It was about me finding a brotherhood of men that would display the utmost interest and accountability in my growth and I in theirs. The process was about me learning how to die to self daily in order to serve my wife adequately. The process was about seeking out one or two mentoring couples that had it right and staying close to them. The process gave me in return a Proverbs 31 woman. The process taught me that I really have a partner who is willing to tackle my goals as our goals. The process taught me to seek first the kingdom of God and His Righteousness, and He has added everything else I desired and more. We allowed God to step in.

So why did she pick me? I agree that my wife saw a plan as well as commitment and drive to succeed. I agree that she saw a love for family unlike she had seen anywhere else in her life. However, God by His design has a lot to accomplish through this marital union. God has a plan for us, and we try to walk the narrow path daily in order to avoid disappointing Him in our journey. As you read this book, you are in His design. We feel it is even more astonishing the number of couples that God has brought into our lives to mentor in marriage or to bring into a renewed relationship with Him. To them, not knowing the road we've traveled in most cases, they see a healthy relationship and family they can emulate. We humbly see severely broken vessels that God was gracious enough to renew for accomplishing His purpose. What do you intend to do with your marital struggles? I dare you to put God and His Word to the test and absolutely seek Him as the answer to marriage challenges. Obey what his word (The Bible) says to the letter, especially about marriage.

CHAPTER SIX:

God's Sovereign Hand Never Loses Its Firm Grip. He Guides Us.

There is a feeling of loneliness that sometimes accompanies the position of the firstborn son; at those times we feel lost and misguided. There is also a heightened feeling of failure and fear that we are letting people down. These scenarios usually come along when we fail to accomplish a task in which we have engaged. Quite regularly, engaging in a task does not affect just us as the firstborn sons. Every project seemingly, and truly in most cases, affects every one that is dependent on us. The loss of work, failure to meet deadlines, investments gone bad, or social failures such as infidelity, all of these have a serious trickle down effect. I would love to tell you, "Oh don't bother…take it like water off a duck's back." But the reality of the situation is, the position of leadership is a very lonely place. A lot is expected of you but for an excellent reason.

God has laid out a great description of the required characteristics. He has also promised His good grace and availability through a never easy or trivial task such as filling your leadership role. In this chapter, I will explore many of these characteristics and promises God has given.

"Oh, Take It Easy. It Is Not That Serious." Is It So…?

Why should we take it easy? Have we not been entrusted with the lives and well being of God's precious children? I don't intend to take God's business as playful business. God has given us a role of leadership over His children. Everyone that depends on us for life and sustenance is so important to God that He chooses to adopt them into His family as a child, much like He saw His Son Jesus Christ.

"For you did not receive a spirit that makes you a slave again to fear, but you received the Spirit of sonship. And by him we cry, 'Abba, Father.' The Spirit himself testifies with our spirit that we are God's children. Now if we are children, then we are heirs—heirs of God and co-heirs with Christ, if indeed we share in his sufferings in order that we may also share in his glory" (Rom. 8:15-17).

Why then do we think that we can afford to pursue our responsibilities of caring for God's children with anything less than the utmost priority? As a matter of fact, it is amazing that He even sees us worthy of the responsibility. Every time I look at my family and realize the trust they place in me I am humbled by the thought that God would see me worthy.

This does not mean that there will not be opportunities to fall short. As a matter of fact we will fall short. Let's just get that out of the way. The beauty of the fall, only in heavenly wisdom, is that we are in the right position to look up to God, visualize, and refocus on His grace. Even better, He is reaching down to pull us back to our feet as a loving father would do for his fallen child. What we do instead is hang our heads, and begin a masterful display of navel-gazing. With our heads hung low, solemnly staring at our navels, we fail to see His outstretched hand. In case you forgot, you are also His child. As any proud father, He wishes to pull you up, dust you off, and set you on your way to ultimate success.

"If you, then, though you are evil, know how to *give good gifts* to your children, how much more will your Father in heaven *give good gifts* to those who ask him!" (Matt. 7:11, italics mine).

So what is this ultimate success for a firstborn son? Make no mistake—a firstborn son is also God's chosen leader. All through Scripture, God specifies the importance He places on the first-born beginning with Christ as the firstborn amongst many brethren. As such, I have to present a description of what our responsibilities as God's leaders looks like. I will not yet describe or directly outline the rules and requirements for the position of firstborn son. But I can paint a pretty close portrait of this role by looking at what God expects of His leaders and overseers at this point.

What does He expect of those that shepherd His flock? What does He expect of those individuals in leadership roles? What are the characteristics or traits that others will look at and easily iden-tify us as protectors of God's most prized possessions? The priests of our respective homes; that is what we are.

"Here is a trustworthy saying: If anyone sets his heart on being an overseer, he desires a noble task. Now the overseer must be above reproach, the husband of but one wife, temperate, self-controlled, respectable, hospitable, able to teach, not given to drunkenness, not violent but gentle, not quarrelsome, not a lover of money. He must manage his own family well and see that his children obey him with proper respect. (If anyone does not know how to manage his own family...)" (1 Tim. 3:1-5).

"Husbands, love your wives, just as Christ loved the church and gave himself up for her to make her holy, cleansing her by the washing with water through the word, and to present her to himself as a radiant church, without stain or wrinkle or any other blemish, but holy and blameless. In this same way, husbands ought to love their wives as their own bodies. He who loves his wife loves himself. After all, no one ever hated his own body, but he feeds and cares for it, just as Christ does the church—for we are members of his body" (Eph. 5:25-30).

As we read these role descriptions, there are a few attributes that are clearly being echoed. These echoes express selflessness, sacrificial living, and yes, that you are a role model. There are many watching you and expecting impeccable character that resembles "holiness and blamelessness."

So, I know the wheels must be spinning uncontrollably in your head. They're spinning so hard and fast there's smoke coming out of your ears, possibly you're even furious at this moment. You are saying, "Zeke, this is an impossible life to live, especially if I am not a pastor or church elder." You are saying, "This stuff about living a life that renders me, much less someone else who is dependent on me, holy and blameless before God, is impractical and ridiculous." Here is another Scripture for you to consider...the key here is *wisdom*. However, it is not wisdom as our society typically describes.

> "We do, however, speak a message of wisdom among the mature, but not the wisdom of this age or of the rulers of this age, who are coming to nothing. No, we speak of God's secret wisdom, a wisdom that has been hidden and that God destined for our glory before time began. None of the rulers of this age understood it, for if they had, they would not have crucified the Lord of glory. However, as it is written: 'No eye has seen, no ear has heard, no mind has conceived what God has prepared for those who love him' but God has revealed it to us by his Spirit" (1 Cor. 2:6-10)

Preference and Significance God Places on the Position of the Firstborn Son

Long before primogeniture was practiced, God has had a significant place in His heart for firstborn sons. Allow me to bring your attention to how our creator sees you, the firstborn son.

Let's explore some specific descriptions on this fact. (See Appendix A for Scriptures referenced below.)

A. God likens the nation of Israel to a firstborn son, His firstborn son. He goes on to say He nurtured that relationship so that His firstborn son will worship Him. Firstborn son, God desires a deliberate relationship of worship from you. (Ex. 4:22-23)

B. God declares an extra desire for ownership upon firstborn sons. He said consecrate (which is to sanctify, bless, set apart, make holy) them to Me. Firstborn son, will you dedicate yourself wholly and solely to the desires of the Father, even as our Lord Jesus Christ (our greatest example) did? (Ex. 13:1-2, Luke 2:23)

C. God desires a special relationship with His firstborn sons. At the designation of the Levites to relational replacement of the firstborn sons in Israel, He lists some key characteristics He seeks from this relationship. He demands purity, a spiritual working relationship, and individuals consecrated or set apart to Him. God has clearly always desired a preferable and uniquely responsible relationship with firstborn sons—one of duty, dependability, and accountability. Now that you know this, are you prepared to accept and honor your place as the firstborn son? (Num. 8:14-19)

D. Fathers, do not rob your firstborn son of his birthright because of favoritism of another and thereby promote the Esau Disorder. He is meant to carry on your legacy and is rightfully and strategically placed as such. He is the first sign of your strength (vigor, strong suit, assets, power). Acknowledge him with your words of affirmation and confirmation, and give him a double portion of your wisdom if not your wealth. That birthright belongs to him. (Deut. 21:15-17)

E. Much like he did with Israel, which is His firstborn son, God is interested in the restoration of wayward relationship. (Jer. 31:9)

F. Our God longs for the provision of deep and prayerful protection of His firstborn son. As such, the grief experience over the loss of a firstborn son (Christ, the One who was pierced) is likened to bitterness. (Zech. 12:10-14)

G. God the Father empowers His firstborn son toward greatness and victorious living. With Christ as the firstborn amongst many brethren, He opens the door as an invitation for us to partake in a life of power, rather than one of worry or defeat. A conqueror defeats, subjugates, vanquishes his captors. Firstborn sons, if we are to follow Christ who is the Firstborn amongst many brethren, we are greater than conquerors. Are you honestly able to voice that to yourself with true conviction? (Rom. 8:28-30)

Firstborn son, the bottom line is this, our God has and will forever have a tender spot on His heart for the position and role we fill. Indeed, there are great responsibilities that come attached to this role and title. The great God of balance also provides incredible preferences and birthrights that we can embrace. So, regardless of the pressures that seem insurmountable, I submit this to you; you are in the hands of Jesus Christ. First, avoid the Esau Disorder. Then, CARPE DIEM (seize the day)! Your God is the great "I AM" (not I Was or I Will). He exists from eternity but operates in the present.

As I spent time revisiting my past and the route that got me where I am today, I'd like to say I had everything to do with it. However, the reality is undoubtedly true to me that God absolutely guided my path. God's only revelation of His plans and intentions for my life were made apparent to me in the presence of His Spirit. It is in His will that I accepted and stepped into His direction for me by faith although I may have questioned with human logic. However, I do not obey with human wisdom or "wisdom of this age." It is very easy to look back and see the relevancy of particular incidents in my life and the preparation gained by the various occurrences.

Firstborn son, do you believe and embrace God's predestined grace upon your life? Or does it seem to be just a cool mythical concept from a Harry Potter movie for you? When it comes to living with God for a lifetime, have you embraced the fact that God is right now preparing you for the great works he has ahead?

"For we are God's workmanship, created in Christ Jesus to do good works, which God prepared in advance for us to do" (Eph. 2:10).

In case you didn't catch it, this is exactly what 1 Corinthians 2:9-10 says (…no eye has seen…). The secret guiding wisdom of God, destined for you long before time began, is revealed to you through the person of Jesus Christ, His Word, and His Spirit. Who knows your inner thoughts better than your spirit that resides within? But God has given us His Spirit (the Promised One, the Comforter) to reside in us so that we can know, understand, and take heed that His secret (mystery) wisdom is best. He reveals that wisdom through His Spirit (see 1 Corinthians 2:10). So, accept His Spirit because if you don't you will miss out on His wisdom.

"The man without the Spirit does not accept the things that come from the Spirit of God, for they are foolishness to him, and he cannot understand them, because they are spiritually discerned" (1 Cor. 2:14).

Allow me to give you a snapshot of how being led by the Holy Spirit over a lifetime unfolds.

- My friends, my parents gave life to me in a great environment (Baptist boarding school). What a wonderful place to live and raise a child. However in the midst of that wonderful place a war broke out. Possessing all reasons (lack of food, numerous tortures and harassments, direct invitations and conscription, and so forth) to pick up an AK-47 rifle during a war, I did not give in by God's guidance.

- I was recruited for college basketball in America directly out of Africa without the coach seeing any video of me playing.

- The simple recommendations from a family the coach never knew prior to that conversation earned me a scholarship. By the way, this family had no connections to high school or college basketball.

- Little did I know when I left Africa on that December morning I would not see my family for what seemed like an eternity (eight years). Nevertheless, the distance was all worth it.

- I avoided encounters with the law and drug pitfalls of numerous friends as an impressionable college athlete.

- I also saw the total restoration and reuniting of my family out of war unharmed.

- I was blessed with a solid collegiate education amidst all the distractions.

- Later on in life, I saw His hand in the restoration of a marriage so bitterly and tragically destroyed.

- Beyond all of this, the current provision of my family is so immeasurably blessed by God, and I can keep on listing blessings.

However, my point is that God has always guided me with His spiritual and biblical wisdom and has always been there during my falls to reach out His hand, pick me up, dust me off, and move me along to His ultimate success for my life. When it comes to leading my family and the upbringing of my firstborn son, Garrison, there is total reliance on the sovereignty of God the Father. His sovereign hand has never lost a firm grip on me nor has He lost a firm grip on you. Do you have a reason or proof to believe that He doesn't have His firm grip on you?

CHAPTER SEVEN:

Dedication of My Firstborn Son– How Will I Guide Him?

I have been tremendously blessed by my heavenly Father who saw it best to make me the firstborn son of my parents Ezechiel, Sr. and Anne. I have an incredibly gifted, passionate, intelligent, and most importantly, faithful wife. I speak of her faithfulness not necessarily to me but first and foremost to our Lord and Savior Jesus Christ. However, I will rave of her faithfulness to me because I am the absolute benefactor of her phenomenal relationship with Jesus Christ. Our marital union has produced two absolute blessings of joy, our children. Our daughter, Haedyn Grace, age four, is fast becoming the princess that blows my mind, and she reflects so much of her mother. If she is to develop the drive, intelligence, and passionate love and faithfulness her mother possesses, my joy concerning her life on this earth will be close to complete. A full completion of my joy rests in her utter relationship, commitment, and service to our Lord and Savior Jesus Christ in her life on this earth.

Then there is my handsome and already incredible and joyful temperament of a son, Garrison Asher, age six months. I have to testify about my beautiful wife once more. I remember when we went into the hospital to perform the ultrasound in hopes of determining the gender of our baby. My wife had spent so much time praying to the Lord that we would be blessed with a son, her gift to me that words could not express. My wife further attests that even on the walk into the hospital and subsequently the ultrasound room, she was convinced that at that last moment if God wanted to change the gender from a girl to a boy, with His miracle and power He could. When we were told that we were indeed having a boy, she let out an intense, tearful, yet joyful scream. I think people in the halls thought something horrific had happened in the room. All I have to go by is the blank and weird stares the nurses on the floor gave us as we left. But I think the smiles on our faces gave away the true sentiment. Yes, that is "the woman You gave me God," and I gladly accept her. It is also important that our God has given us a firstborn son to carry on the legacy of the Bambolo name.

I have to ask myself…Firstborn son, what DNA do you intend to pass on to your firstborn son? What architectural blueprint will you give him, allowing him to socially impact his generation spiritually and socially for Christ? Firstborn son, will you rob him of his birthright or give him the necessary tools to eliminate the Esau Disorder? Firstborn son, is it not your God–given duty to nurture him into the Proverbs 2 son?

The Esau Disorder or the Proverbs 2 Son

Why does God put such emphasis on the position of the first-born son? Primogeniture is the preferential and exclusive right of inheritance that is provided by law, and at times customarily, given to the eldest son. Primogeniture is not as common a practice as it was many years ago. Times have changed indeed, but many of the fringe benefits and expectations still exist. They simply exist for the most part in principle and not always formally exercised.

There was a twofold reason for such a practice. It was done in an attempt to keep the estate and other desired institutions of the deceased in one piece rather than separated. It was also practiced or established in an effort to confirm the importance of age seniority of the eldest son within the social hierarchy.

Today it is not so common to find parents committing all of their estate to one child, especially the firstborn son. More frequently, in recent times, last wills and testaments divide inheritances in many instances equivalently among all surviving children.

I touch on this fact to accentuate how important a role the firstborn son has held for centuries and the grave expectation to perform that his parents placed on him. Many men have been thrilled to accept and carry on legacies from generations hundreds of years before their birth. Are we as worthy or eager to fill such a hierarchical role anymore? Do we believe that without question, the role of the firstborn son has been so minimized that we unflinchingly take the role of Esau (see Genesis 25:32-33) quite regularly? More than often we willingly give away our birthright succumbing temptations of this world. As you have probably noticed by now I have coined a new phrase for this behavior and call it the **Esau Disorder**.

What is the Esau Disorder? Esau, a masterful outdoorsman comes in from a day of hunting and is absolutely famished. Jacob, a home body and mommy's boy has been home cooking up some incredibly tasty stew. I am not saying every man that cooks is a mommy's boy, or that being a mommy's boy is wrong. Scripture does describe that Jacob was fond of his mother and vice versa. As Esau arrives he smells the stew and comes in to Jacob asking for some stew in order to subdue his massive hunger. Essentially Jacob says, "Sell me your birthright then I will give you some stew." Esau proceeds to verbalize this, "What good is the birthright if I am going to die of starvation anyway?" Jacob says "Well, sell it then." Esau does. He sells his right as the firstborn son to his younger brother for a bowl of stew! He sells his right to carry on the legacy of his father, Isaac, as the firstborn son to his brother over some hunger pains that could have probably been contained with a cup of water until he prepared something. We have all been starved before. I have actually been starved for multiple days in the midst of a war. Esau's attitude was an absolute careless one that showed no regard for God's design on his life.

Firstborn son, do you need an example of a modern day Esau? There are many all around us. Answer this: How many firstborn sons have chosen the wayward lifestyle of family neglect, drunkenness, drug abuse, domestic violence, pornography, (insert your sin here), only to find a younger son willing to step in to uphold and carry on his father's legacy? Sometimes a family in desperate need has to go the route of an adoptee to find the legacy bearer. Firstborn son, if you fit this profile, you have exercised the Esau Disorder. You have displayed the same carelessness Esau did and have no regard for God's design on your life.

Do we understand how gravely this disorder affects our homes and subsequently our society? Taking a look at the topic of cultural apologetics and the effects of feminism on America, here are few adverse conditions brought about by this cancerous movement:

- Men don't know how to be men anymore.

- We no longer make it our duty to teach our sons how to be men. It is the school's, youth pastor's, coach's, or someone else's job. Some men shamefully leave this task up to the so-called "school of hard knocks," which in most cases is taught by their son's peer friendships.

- If we teach our sons to be too masculine it will be offensive to others and uncomfortable for them.

- Men are uncomfortable being men.

- They are uncomfortable being fathers, providers, heads of homes, and spiritual leaders of today's families.

- Men are failing to fill the role of leading their family

- Sons and future fathers are not seeing what being a man truly looks like.

- Daughters and future wives are not seeing what character-istics to look for in a man and future husband.

I believe the above listed cultural apologetic concerns express some extremely valid observations in order to expose our societal flaws. But I'll have to add that the Esau Disorder has a lot to do with it as well. Men just flat out have no regard for their God-given birthright, firstborn son or not. The Esau Disorder is highly important for firstborn sons but applies to sons in general as well. Furthermore, the eradication of the Esau Disorder has to be approached in a personal and introspective manner. One does not need a ten-step plan to change or correct the situation; it is a choice. Firstborn son, just like Esau could not blame anyone for his choice, we cannot either. Firstborn son, just as Esau had to deal with the consequences of his decision…, so do we.

> "When Esau was forty years old, he married Judith daughter of Beeri the Hittite, and also Basemath daughter of Elon the Hittite. They were a source of grief to Isaac and Rebekah" (Gen. 26:34-35).

Esau doesn't seem to possess the characteristics of a Proverbs 2 son. Do you? Oh, but there is hope…

Upcoming Spiritual Dedication of My Firstborn Son

The ceremony of the dedication of our son is a call to us the parents to raise him in a godly manner.

> "Train a child in the way he should go, and when he is old he will not turn from it" (Prov. 22:6).

> "Fathers, do not exasperate your children; instead, bring them up in the training and instruction of the Lord" (Eph. 6:4).

The ceremony is performed before the church body and usually with the support of immediate family members. A prayer is offered to God in the presence of many witnesses (the congregation) that we, as parents, vow to do all within our power to raise the child in the way of the Lord. Our church family also comes along beside us in a commitment to be good examples for the child and live a godly example. One day in the future, any one of our fellow parishioners may be the conduit by which that child comes to know our Lord Jesus Christ personally, if not by us his parents. At the current age of six months, Garrison is by far too young to understand the need and nature of a personal relationship with Jesus. Therefore, baptism, which is a new believer's personal and conscious decision to be symbolically buried and resurrected with Jesus Christ into a renewed life and way of thinking is not applicable. An infant is not yet capable of such volition.

Weeks in advance, my wife made the arrangements for the dedication of my firstborn son at our church. I was well aware the day was fast approaching and went about my daily routines without much distraction until the week before.

It seems the reality and magnitude of the occasion began to take its effect. All of a sudden, my work week seemed to have all of these uncontrollable glaring issues. Here I was, in a bit of some award winning navel-gazing, as if God had not done the work in me already, with and through many years of preparation. Furthermore, He has given me all sorts of instructions in His Scripture of how to raise His firstborn son that He has blessed me with.

But really, why was I so uncomfortable about this task? What obstacles do I see that will hinder me from achieving this goal? Am I being over dramatic and simply creating a false sense of quandary? I now have the task of developing my firstborn son for a social environment that is by far more continuously degenerate than that of my childhood. The rules of engagement are aggressively being changed with no regard for true traditional family values. The signs and consequences of these blatant disregards are vividly apparent all around us. For the sake of our sons and daughters we cannot stand by idly. I do not plan to stand by idly, so here is a view of our game plan.

In a Very Few Short Years, Our World Will Be Much More Dangerous.

I had a conversation with my brother just yesterday about the dangers our children face, even from within our family. A few short years ago my parents dedicated me in Washington Chapel Baptist Church (Liberia, West Africa). While raising us, our parents were more concerned about the physical dangers we faced. The mental and psychological dangers that we are faced with today were present but definitely not as mainstream as they are today. There was a greater sensitivity toward good and evil or moral absolutes. Our children, especially my son, will face much worse dangers in the years to come. He will face worse dangers because we have eroded the foundations of moral absolutes and left our societal structures crumbling. My brother's question was, "Why would you not trust your child's safety in the hands of a family member who does not have the same social and spiritual values but loves the child greatly as family nonetheless?" I wouldn't trust them because as he stated, our "social and spiritual values" are not the same. Many of us tend to minimize this incredibly critical pillar of our children's development. That is a sad, sad mistake.

Do you remember the old African proverb "It takes a village to raise a child"? Thank God that I am African and lived this proverb. My parents' world of raising a child as recently as the 1970s and 1980s was such that the village did raise the child. I remember taking a few spankings from a neighbor that was as close as family to me. More importantly, my parents trusted the motives of the neighbors' value systems and intentions. How is that working for you and me today? Think about it further. Are parents even comfortable uttering the old African proverb? We are generally the same people and have chosen the same neighborhoods to raise our kids in with similar value systems or else we would be living worlds apart, right? I am afraid not.

The sad reality for parents is that the village has failed us terribly. The mental or psychological dangers are by far more damaging than most physical ones our children face. Most physical dangers are temporal. However, the detrimental psychological persuasions tend to be life-lasting barring severely-life impacting consequences that have a chance to reshape their thinking. Here is a short list of some things that have seen drastic changes of influence on children, especially in schools (where they spend a great number of life impacting hours) since the 1970s.

1) Dress code—from gothic to sagging pants revealing underwear. What happened to proper dress etiquette?

2) Addressing superiors formally as Mr. or Miss or Mrs.—no lines of distinction between peers and elders.

3) Parental meddling—are kids no longer capable of having respectable and accountable discussions with teachers and staff anymore?

4) Faculty/staff misconduct—how do these personalities get into positions of authority without administrative accountability exposing them. Are we as parents doing enough to teach our children moral absolutes so that they do not easily fall prey and are able to quickly sound the alarm that saves them and their peers.

5) GSA (Gay Straight Alliance)—immoral and unnatural behavior has and now continues to demand equality with moral and natural behavior. A promotional sign at a local high school at the beginning of the school year read, "Please join us for another year of spreading the radical doctrine of tolerance."

6) Biblical phobias—for a country whose original constitution and social value systems are intimately laced with Christian principles and whose founding fathers emphatically stated that "religion and morality" are the foundation and core of its existence or else there would be utter chaos. Why is there such call for the separation of church and state (Christianity out of schools, because it surely isn't "religion out of schools"? Yet we wonder why America is losing its luster in the eyes of the world.

7) ...and more indeed.

However, we continue to wonder why there is a massive growth of insensitivity in our media outlets and the likes. Media outlets are a great source of education and entertainment. I cannot stress to you enough how much access to a television in Africa gave me a great sense of preparation and expectation for life in America. Media opens a great viewing portal to the world's great many cultures, if I may use my Star Trek analogy. But what is the limit of our sacrifice, and how do we determine what crosses the line of our duties as protectors of our children?

More graphic and anti-child friendly movies on our television are broadcast directly into our homes. Even when we decide to heavily monitor the shows that are allowable, the commercials for other network programming that are aired during the breaks are worse than what we've already chosen to disallow for our children! What happened to family sensitive comedies like *The Cosby Show, Good Times, Different Strokes, and Full House?* Instead "kid friendly" Disney television portrays *The Wizards of Waverly Place* (witchcraft), *The Suite Life* (materialism), and made for television movies on mean, nasty, and vindictive teenage girl catfights. These are being forced upon us as normal behavior of our day and suitable for children.

Some say, "We are progressive thinkers these days." Really, is it so? Did we not know those kinds of personalities and behaviors (witchcraft, materialism, and so on) existed when we watched the child-friendly comedies and cartoons? Yes, we did. Now, we are just giving our children a free pass to be those personalities and act out those behaviors in the name of progressive thinking. No wonder why we have the six issues listed above and more that plague our schools. No wonder why the village has failed us when it comes to raising a child. No wonder why our community value systems are so distant even though we are next door neighbors and relatives of the same blood.

It is not just that "a mind is a terrible thing to waste." What is sad but true and my description of the situation is that a wasted mind loses all sense of direction (its own moral north) and tragically spins out of control to its own demise. Why do we have more violent crimes especially from unsuspecting individuals (those in whom the distinction of evil or good is difficult)? Why do we have more radical fundamentalist religious intolerance (such as terrorists, both domestic and international)? Why do we have such erosion of elementary value systems that govern true community (such as the village)? Have we counted the number of wasted minds in our midst lately? Have we counted how many wasted minds we continue to develop? Can we not see that we are losing control and spinning into our own demise? The world is dangerous now, but it is fast becoming a far more dangerous place for my son. My children will know and learn that there are moral absolutes by which they are to align their lives. There is a roadmap that has a very narrow road with few options but leads them directly to the truth (see Matthew 7:13-14). A fact that is even more disheartening about the wide and destructive road stated in the Scripture verse mentioned above is this: The people in law enforcement, government, and other officials we have trusted to protect us and our children willingly walk this destructive road as you will see in the next segment

The Devil Is a Liar

As I am writing this book, I have just been informed by a very close friend of an incident in his home. It clearly depicts our society's attempt or agenda to feminize men and fathers. Society's agenda is to promote the Esau Disorder and continue to create an innumerable amount of wasted minds. Society is the world, and the prince of this world, the prince of darkness is the devil. He seeks to render us instruments of wickedness, rather than God's instruments of righteousness. If you don't believe me or didn't know this, open your Bible and read Romans 6. Firstborn son, how far are you willing to go when fighting for the birthright of your firstborn son?

My friend (whom I will call Edson) had a situation with his sixteen-year-old son (whom I will call Dante) that required an absolute stand as a father. Dante is a firstborn son that has been raised in a Christian home with a mother and father that are highly committed believers. He has been in the halls of the church since birth, serves as an usher, and has a wonderful nucleus of immediate family members and extended church family that live exemplary lives. As most young men do, lately he has been making some wayward decisions (smoking, defiance, and so forth) due to peer influence and the lure to run with the wrong but so-called "cool" crowd.

Dante and a friend decided to borrow his father's bicycles to make a run without asking. Unfortunately for Dante, he was at a place with the wrong crowd and eventually got his father's bicycles stolen. Dante and his friend were a good long distance away from home and rather than bear the consequence of walking home or seeking other avenues of solving the matter, they decided to steal two bicycles from other people. When Edson approached his son about the error and horrible decision he had made in an effort to shape the behavior of his firstborn son, Dante became very defiant and refused to show sufficient remorse concerning the situation. Edson instituted a punishment stating he would sell Dante's video games in order to get the money to repurchase bicycles. He instructed Dante to bring the games to his room. Dante chose the absolute defiant road, a detour from the roadmap that has been instilled in him by his parents and surroundings all his life. Dante chose to do so in a mode of complete confrontational defiance to his father regardless of repeated warnings.

Edson had to respond to a son who had now riskily pushed the limits. Dante threatened his understanding of the birthright he possesses. He risked rejecting the hierarchy of authority that exists within the father and son relationship and typically feeds his reverence for the family inheritance and legacy. Dante displayed a confrontational rejection of his father's outpour of wisdom and a serious threat to embrace the Esau Disorder. Last but not least, Edson had come face-to-face with the devil that intended to destroy what has been an honestly beautiful and healthy home. Faced with the challenge far greater than simply a disobedient son, Edson's response was to take his belt and give his boy a good spanking back to reality. One of the devil's greatest tricks is to use our closest loves to render us powerless. I got one of those spankings as well in my teenage years, therefore I can understand and appreciate the education and restoration that was in session.

"I will be his father, and he will be my son. When he does wrong, I will punish him with the rod of men, with floggings inflicted by men" (2 Sam. 7:14).

"He who spares the rod hates his son, but he who loves him is careful to discipline him" (Prov. 13:24).

"Folly is bound up in the heart of a child, but the rod of discipline will drive it far from him" (Prov. 22:15).

"The rod of correction imparts wisdom, but a child left to himself disgraces his mother" (Prov. 29:15).

Dante finally submitted and brought the video games to his father's room as requested. However, the devil through our society has fabricated a great lie to our kids and families. The lie is the sense of entitlement, which in turn breeds arrogance within us. While Edson and his wife were in bed late at night, she encouraged him to go and make sure their son was secured in his room. When Edson came into the halls of his home, he found Dante roaming and on his way out of the home. Dante had been in the habit recently of sneaking out of the home to congregate with the wrong group of friends. Edson asked him where he was going, and he said he was leaving the home. Edson told him he wasn't allowed and Dante threatened to call the police on his father. Edson said, "Go ahead." Dante called the police, and three squad cars came to their home late that night. (Their home had no records of any prior disturbances.) The police proceeded to investigate and went as far as asking Edson's wife if she wanted to press charges on Edson! She responded, "Absolutely not. We simply have a disobedient son." Edson told them the full story, and the police, hiding behind the law, decided they had to take Edson to jail for the night because he hit is son with a belt.

Is it me or does the court system or law appear to be a clown upside down on its head? We have become greatly intelligent as a people in the name of "progressive thinking," that our decisions and laws when measured against common sense are shockingly dumb.

Edson is a father who has absolutely no records of criminal activity. He has desired to live nothing but the life of a godly man; he is an extremely productive citizen (husband, father, and business owner). Edson chose to discipline his firstborn son. If Edson chose to leave Dante in the behavior just portrayed, wasn't Dante sure to become a statistic in this country's prison systems? How many families out there can now identify with their sons displaying similar defiant behavior one too many times? How many families did not do enough to discourage the direction they were heading and now find those sons dead, incarcerated, or unable to lead stable and productive lives? Tell me then why Edson now has a criminal profile for standing up for his family.

Edson did an amazing job of filling his role as a representation of Jesus Christ for his family. He had to die to himself and take the abuse from both his society and his child in an effort to be the sacrifice. Jesus Christ is the sacrifice whom our society abuses and we abuse as well, regardless of His desire and effort to free us and make us instruments of righteousness. Observing Edson's choices, how much are you willing to endure to protect your firstborn son from the destructive detours of life? Dante, after watching his father's actions, was terribly sorry for the choices he made and is, for the time being, resubmitting himself obediently to his parents' wishes. The cost of sacrifice is high, but the result rather immediate or long term is priceless.

As I spoke to Edson about the incident, his criminal record, his family, and more importantly his firstborn son, the phrase he uttered repeatedly is, "The Devil is a liar." In other words, he has resounded never to let the paralyzing fear imposed on us by the prince of this world (and his manipulation of our governments, its laws, and its people, we the voters) defeat his desire to be the father God has ordained him to be.

World Powers, Conspiracy Theories, Cults, Occults and the One Universe

It is all one big blur it seems if you stop and listen to many a misguided religion, churches, conspiracy theorists, world powers seeking domination, and how they all intertwine into the great cosmos, the great power of the universe. The master manipulator and counterfeiter (the Devil) has really done a number on mankind. He has done a masterful job of creating so many options for distraction from the one true God and His Trinitarian nature. Firstborn son, if you do not have a firm footing on which to stand, or one to pass on the legacy to *your* firstborn son, it is absolutely impossible to avoid the traps that so vividly demand our attention. Let me elaborate on a few examples.

I do not have the information I need to make adequate decisions sometimes concerning most issues that are domestic or world impacting. It seems the people that have the privilege of receiving pertinent information choose to withhold the complete details. They give bits and pieces in an attempt to manipulate the outcome. It is a tug of war for world power and domination both domestically and internationally. *Who do we trust and what is our line of discernment?*

Here are some examples that are renowned media sources that very regularly leave me baffled, just as you are I am sure. I happened to be writing this book at the time of a big debate regarding US President Obama's national healthcare plan. See if you can determine the truth about what America really desires on healthcare in response to the president's speech from these poll reports.

"Poll: Support for Health Care Reform Tepid as More Americans Oppose Legislation

...Just 37 percent of Americans support the pending legislation, which is expected to be picked up again as Congress returns to session Tuesday following a month-long recess. A slightly larger number — 39 percent — want their congressmen to vote against the bill..."[14]

'Poll: Public Disapproval of 'Obamacare' Jumps to 52 Percent

Public disapproval of President Obama's handling of health care has jumped to 52 percent, according to an Associated Press-GfK poll...

The grade people give Obama on health care also has worsened since July, when just 43 percent disapproved of his work on the issue...

Forty-nine percent say they oppose the health over-haul plans being considered by Congress, compared to just 34 percent who favor them."[15]

"

WASHINGTON (CNN) — Two out of three Americans who watched President Barack Obama's health care reform speech Wednesday night favor his health care plans — a 14-point gain among speech-watchers, according to a CNN/Opinion Research Corporation national poll of people who tuned into Obama's address Wednesday night to a joint session of Congress.

Sixty-seven percent of people questioned in the survey say they support Obama's health care reform proposals that the president outlined in his address, with 29 percent opposed.

The audience for the speech appears to be more Democratic than the U.S. population as a whole. Because of this, the results may favor Obama simply because more Democrats than Republicans tune into the speech. The poll surveyed the opinions of people who watched Wednesday night's speech, and does not reflect the views of all Americans."[16]

"CNN Spins Poll Following Obama Speech Favoring Pro-Abortion Health Care Bill

Washington, DC (LifeNews.com) — CNN has earned itself significant criticism following a poll it conducted after President Barack Obama's speech touting the pro-abortion health care bills. CNN manipulated the number of Republicans and Democrats in the poll to make it appear the speech went over well with the American public. 'Two out of three Americans who watched President Barack Obama's health care reform speech Wednesday night favor his health care plans — a 14-point gain among speech-watchers,' CNN trumpeted today.

'Sixty-seven percent of people questioned in the survey say the support Obama's health care reform proposals that the president outlined in his address,' the news services claimed.

However, at the bottom of its news story on its own survey, CNN admits to polling more than twice as many Democrats as Republicans."[17]

All of these reports are about the exact same issue, the exact same speech, on the healthcare bill. How is it possible for the media outlets to have such differences in results and the views of one people (Americans)? Can we not conduct or at least set standards for an educated poll with a fair mix of constituents from both sides of the issue? Better yet, if we are aware that our polls are slanted, why publish them or talk about them in post-speech interviews? Is it a ploy to muddy the water by presenting faulty information and later retract statements on claims of error when challenged? The media outlets report with their biases rather than objectivity. Fair and balanced reporting appears to no longer be of any importance. What happened to the decency of honesty by saying, "We do not have those figures yet"? Is utilizing clear discretion for proper release of information in honor of the profession an option anymore? Not if there are no societal moral absolutes, even for the free press and its purposes.

"The Freedom of press includes more than merely serving as a 'neutral conduit of information between the people and their elected leader or as a neutral form of debate'...

In today's free world freedom of press is the heart of social and political intercourse. The press has now assumed the role of the public educator making formal and non-formal education possible in a large scale particularly in the developing world, where television and other kinds of modern communication are not still available for all sections of society. The purpose of the press is to advance the public interest by publishing facts and opinions without which a democratic electorate

[Government] cannot make responsible judgments. Newspapers being purveyors of news and views having a bearing on public administration very often carry material which would not be palatable to Governments and other authorities."[18]

I do not list the various outlets in an attempt to discredit any media outlet. I do not possess the expertise or the complete information to do so, far from that. Unfortunately, I am also far removed from the halls of Washington, DC, nor able to visit every town hall and tea party discussion conducted. I do not have the time to research and find the details after a busy day's work, but I wish to take advantage of the news media outlets (television, radio, or Internet). The purpose for displaying these segments of articles is this: How does an objective party like me rely on the articles above to make an informed decision? The political scene seems more like a propaganda tug of war with misinformed or limited information designed to sway votes rather than rightfully serve the people of this country's interest. *Who do we trust, and what is our line of discernment?*

To further complicate the issue, firstborn son, while our surroundings and that of our sons' future leaderships are being hijacked by personalities with selfish ambitions rather than led by people who have a genuine interest of others, God's people, and children, we turn to faith to seek fulfillment. Sadly, in most cases we are gravely disappointed to see how empty our religion has become.

Deep inside each of us we feel a natural calling of a supernatural power greater than the common human spirit. I guarantee you that yearning is not the pull of Carl Sagan's depiction of the cosmos. In the depths of our soul we feel the urge daily of something lacking inside. Even in the so-called Dark Continent of Africa, our traditional or bush schools for centuries (long before Christian missionaries) have pointed to the need to fill that void empty of something evidently supernatural. It is the pull of or the yearning for the Creator, not the created. See if these Scriptures get you thinking a bit.

"God said, Let Us [Father, Son, and Holy Spirit] make mankind in *Our image*, after *Our likeness*, and let them have *complete authority* over the fish of the sea, the birds of the air, the [tame] beasts, and *over all of the earth*, and over everything that creeps upon the earth. So God created man in His own image, in the image and likeness of God He created him; male and female He created them" (Gen. 1:26-27, italics mine, AMP).

"And the Lord God planted a garden toward the east, in Eden [delight]; and there He put the man whom He had formed (framed, constituted)" (Gen. 2:8, AMP).

"And they heard the sound of the Lord God walking in the garden in the cool of the day, and Adam and his wife hid themselves from the presence of the Lord God among the trees of the garden" (Gen. 3:8, AMP)

"So Paul, standing in the center of the Areopagus [Mars Hill meeting place], said: Men of Athens, I perceive in every way [on every hand and with every turn I make] that you are most religious or very reverent to demons. For as I passed along and carefully observed your objects of worship, I came also upon an altar with this inscription, To the unknown god. Now what you are already worshiping as unknown, this I set forth to you. The God Who produced and formed the world and all things in it, being Lord of heaven and earth, does not dwell in handmade shrines. Neither is He served by human hands, as though He lacked anything, for it is He Himself Who gives life and breath and all things to all [people]. And He made from one [common origin, one source, one blood] all nations of men to settle on the face of the earth, having definitely determined [their] allotted periods of time and the fixed boundaries of their habitation (their settlements, lands, and abodes), So that they should seek God, in the hope that they might feel after Him and find Him, although He is not far from each one of us" (Acts 17:22-27, AMP).

I am sensing here as I read these Old and New Testament Scriptures ("concentrating and connecting the Scriptures" as a good friend of mine would say), that God created man, His masterpiece positioned in His most delighted place physically and authoritatively, for intimate and daily fellowship with Him.

For centuries, men, much like we are, have tried to fill that urge or need with countless things. We seek fillers like power, wealth, rage, fame, sex, drugs, children, wives, concubines, work…and the list goes on. But we know and clearly feel there is something missing. Religion, cults, occults, and conspiracy theorists step in with a fierce battle for yours and my sons' and daughters' souls against true Christianity.

What is the difference between the two sides? Why have I chosen to group religion, cults, occults, and conspiracy theorists? If your church, or those of your religious affiliation, evidently appears to you as demanding of set of rules, regulations, traditions, rituals, self-reliant efforts, and anything of the sort as an attempt to earn salvation or pursue God, turn and run. All you have is religion and there is no substance. Religion is primarily based on man's attempt to reach God on such human created terms. You will never be able to do enough. You'll be asked to work to earn your salvation, whereas God has provided salvation as a free gift based on man's public proclamation and the condition of the heart (see Romans 10:9). Briefly reflect on our earlier discussion of a godly man and godly living as opposed to just a Christian man from chapter 5.

Christianity, on the other hand, starts and ends with Christ. As you read in Scripture earlier, God created man for intimate fellowship. At the fall of the original parents, Adam and Eve who were God's masterpiece, He began His endeavor to reach and restore man; God reached to man with the offer of the free gift of salvation. This is what that looks like. Immediately upon the fall, the result of sin by man, God shed the blood of His pure creation to cover and protect man (see Genesis 3:21). As life unfolds following that incident and all through the Old Testament, via the tabernacle and the priests, the only acceptable atonement for sin was the blood sacrifice of the purest available animal (usually the firstborn). The animal literally died in the place of the human that should have died for committing the sin. In the process of the sacrifice, which involved the cutting of the throat, the human was instructed to put his hand on the head of the animal. This was a sincere attempt to directly identify with the life that was being taken in one's place. But God took no pleasure in that (see Psalm 40:6-8 and Micah 6:6-8). As such, He decided to send forth the ultimate pure blood sacrifice, His sinless Son Jesus Christ whose blood overrides and supersedes any sacrifice that can ever be given once and for all. Imagine your hand on the head of Jesus Christ through all of the pains and burdens of the crucifixion; that is where it should be in order to understand and internalize His sacrifice for you and me. Imagine feeling Him flinch with every strike or blow He receives. Imagine feeling the tension and strain in His body with every strike of the nails in His hand and feet. Imagine feeling Him shake His head in sorrow and disappointment at every insult or mock hurled at Him. God offers His Son as a sacrifice graciously and freely—the true symbol of His hand reaching out to us and not us working to attain Him. Therefore, all that is required of us is salvation by grace through faith (see Ephesians 2:8-9).

If you have never truly accepted Jesus Christ as your Lord and Savior, you can do so right at this moment. Pray this sincere prayer:

> *Lord, I know that I am a sinner. I believe You sent Your Son, Jesus Christ to die on the cross for my sins, and I receive salvation by grace through faith. I repent of my sins, and I ask for and accept not only the gift and power of His death and resurrection but that He will live in me and renew my mind to His way of thinking. Amen!*

If you have sincerely prayed that prayer, you are now a child of God and now have salvation. It is a gift that can never be taken away from you. (See Romans 10:8-13, 12:1-2.)

However firstborn, we fall prey to the traps and snares so easily because we are not sure of where we stand. Our churches are barely differentiated from cults who are claiming you can have anything you want and that God wants you to have anything you want by simply invoking positive thinking. Remove the name of God from the mission or doctrinal statement of many churches and you have a cult. Add God back in and you have many of our religion-driven, materialistic, modern day churches where it appears (seems as if) God cannot move even an insect into action. However, our God has proven his omnipotence from the beginning by His creation. What's sad but true is that many of these churches are miles wide in size (people), but no more than an inch thick in depth (theology). These churches are not practicing true Christianity. *With God, character trumps comfort.*

In addition, other cults weave in terribly misguided information that the uniqueness of Jesus Christ, who is described in the Holy Bible, is as historically cookie-cutter as age-old religious leaders come. These cults allege that the Holy Bible in its expressions of the uniqueness of Christ copied age-old myths that have been told of many religious leaders long before Jesus Christ. They assert that the Bible's accounts of a virgin birth, the star of Bethlehem, the Christmas story, twelve disciples, among others are all common themes propagated by so many religious icons and as such are easily copied by the Bible. Strangely however, they choose to directly discredit none of those other religious fakes but Jesus Christ. I wonder why…? To garner additional support for their claims, they utilize the scare tactics of conspiracy theories surrounding world disasters to point toward economic and military domination of a select few. All of this is simply to propagate their true message that there is no God and that the universe or cosmos is the source of energy and the ultimate key to life.

I wonder why these positive thinking cults and religions never proactively speak of the adverse effects followers experience when things go awry in their doctrines and teachings. Is it because the easy answer to such a difficult situation is blaming the subject for not engaging enough positive thinking or enough faith in the system? If the universe is such a powerful source of energy to create and sustain life and worth such heralded spiritual worship for intelligent design, why don't these cults have a unique logical explanation of its origin, much less its destination? The Bible does because this great creation did not just come out of nothing. Yes, science and the Bible can co-exist, and as a matter of fact science is in the Bible (see Psalm 19:1-4). It is truly and growingly evident that the farther we look (telescope) into space, and the deeper we look into the cell (microscope), the heavens declare the glory of God and the works of his hands. Unlike the limitations of scientist of old, scholars in recent years have the equipment to look into the mechanism of the human cell and absolutely refute the claims that the order of life came from random chaos. In other words, the "Big Bang" is a big bust. *Again, who do we trust and what is our line of discernment?*

Do We Guide Them or Train Up Navigators?

As parents, we make the mistake of thinking we ought to guide our sons and children. We fail to realize that a guide (tour, fishing, hunting, and so forth) has to be there with you every step of the way. It is impossible for us to be there at every step of our sons' lives. However, by training, preparing, teaching, instructing, and mentoring them and providing the proper roadmap for them, they are safe from deviation (see Proverbs 22:6). They can always consult, review, and study the map and see where they should go. This way we don't have to be the ever-present guide.

My very good friend and a wonderful author, Dr. Karl I. Payne, has some phenomenal information in his "Transferable Cross Training" material that I will burrow to frame this segment of my discussion. These statements clearly depict the extent to which our societies have deteriorated. Yet the proponents of such degenerate thoughts spin it well enough to give their motive a positive label such as "progressive thinking." Karl states, "The society we live in is no longer post-Christian; it is anti-Christian. We live in what is now referred to as the post-modern era." Here are a few of the descriptive proofs he presents to describe our society's descent into post-modernism.[19]

Ethical Theism: circa 400 BC-1200 AD

Right and wrong are absolute and unchanging. God is the giver and ultimate basis for (T)ruth and the source and measure of all (t)ruths. Ethical Theism represents the philosophical foundation for Aristotelian logic and Western thinking.

Darwinism: 1800s-1960s

Materialistic Naturalism can account for everything. Faith should be placed in Rationality (ability of humans to understand world), Empiricism (knowledge gained through the senses), and in Technological achievement rather than in God

Post-Modernism: 1960s-2000s

There is no unifying (T)ruth. Truth is relative. Follow your feelings, follow your heart. If dogs run free, so should we. Something does not have to be rational, logical, analytically consistent nor empirically testable to be true.

Here are a couple of additional statements from post-modernism Karl has in his material on the subject matter:

- Truth is created by communities and culture and is only true in and for that specific community and culture.

- Any person, culture, system, or statement claiming to be objectively true or which unfavorably judges the values, beliefs, lifestyles, and truth claims of others is a power play and an attempt of one culture to dominate another.

A few pages ago I mentioned a GSA (Gay Straight Alliance) promotional poster that hung at the beginning of the school year at a local high school. The key word that you and I have to focus on was boldly and pointedly used in that poster. Here it is again:

"Please join us for another year of spreading the radical doctrine of tolerance."

The key word here is *tolerance*. With the use of the word *tolerance*, our society, homes, high schools, colleges, jobs, and media outlets have been strategically hijacked. Out of sensitivity toward being called names such as bigot or intolerant, we have willfully embraced the Esau Disorder and draped it over our children without even flinching at the thought. We have allowed the word *tolerance* to be redefined. *Tolerance* is defined as "sympathy or indulgence for beliefs or practices *differing from or conflicting with one's own*." (italics mine).[20] In other words, what is happening is clearly wrong and possibly morally absurd. We choose to accept the behavior although they are clearly aware we disapprove of such behavior. However, we can and are clearly entitled to choose not to accept it as well. That decision to not accept does not entitle them to label Christians insensitive. After all, we are the morally and humanly right party in this discussion for as long as history dictates. But even if we are labeled, we have to stand for the sake of our sons and daughters.

The new version of tolerance has come to be known as the view that all values, beliefs, lifestyles, and truth claims are equal. In other words, *out of the fear of hurting or offending someone, there can be no "moral absolutes," only "moral relativisms."* I'm afraid I can't accept that, moral absolutes, especially Scriptural ones, are paramount in my world.

Who Do We Trust and What Is Our Line of Discernment? The Answer Is Clear.

Firstborn son, the proper training and education on yours and my sons for a lifetime of navigating the proper roadmap is by far more important than any name calling or bruised ego that we may receive. When it comes to the moral absolutes of life as it pertains to the biblical foundations and principles that have guided me accurately for thirty-eight years as a firstborn son, I am intolerant, and I am a bigot in the eyes of society as it holds an unbiblical worldview.

Here is a baffling truth... the Holy Bible has been around for thousands of years. It is overwhelmingly the most sold book ever, and it has never required editing or augmenting of its content due to the challenge of its fundamental truth. The many men who wrote the Bible could not have been humanly inspired only. Man's nature is naturally innate and selfish. On the contrary, each man had to be inspired by God through the power of His Holy Spirit. The greatest proof of this is the fact that the underlying and foundational teaching of Scripture instructs us to pursue the glorification of God and the service of our fellow man. This outward rather than inward and selfish focus on service is completely contrary to man's natural inclination. The Holy Bible is the final and complete manuscript (see Revelation 22:18-19) and requires no additions or enhancements. Yet, it bears an answer or perspective for every question or situation I am faced with, both positive and negative, good or evil.

On the other hand, the other sources (religion, cults, media, society, and so forth) that have a design to impact my life cannot compare to the historicity of the Holy Bible. Key doctrinal truths they bear are fluid and constantly changing when hard pressed for answers. Most importantly, the obvious goal of these sources is always manmade and inward only for self-edification and self-improvement. Pause for a moment, and consider our earlier discussions on cults, positive thinking, conspiracy theories, church traditions, and requirements.

As historical as the Holy Bible is, it warns us even in this day and age (the post-modern era) of the dangers. We are instructed to stand firm against deceit and false teachings that claim equality. We are to stand firm against this new tolerance.

"And I will keep on doing what I am doing in order to cut the ground from under those who want an opportunity to be considered equal with us in the things they boast about. For such men are false apostles, deceitful workmen, masquerading as apostles of Christ. And no wonder, for Satan himself masquerades as an angel of light. It is not surprising, then, if his servants masquerade as servants of righteousness. Their end will be what their actions deserve" (2 Cor. 11:12-15).

"Then we will no longer be infants, tossed back and forth by the waves, and blown here and there by every wind of teaching and by the cunning and craftiness of men in their deceitful scheming. Instead, speaking the truth in love, we will in all things grow up into him who is the Head, that is, Christ" (Eph. 4:14-15).

The roadmap or ideology that I have to teach my firstborn son to navigate and avoid countless traps and pitfalls, since I will not be there to guide him for most of his journey, is the Word of God, the Holy Bible. There are rules with finality in an ever-changing world. You must do the same. The question is, "Will you?" Or is earned income, fantasy football, reality TV, scientific research, philanthropic work, drug use, night of drinking with the boys/girls, or (insert your idol here), all of these distractions from the Truth our world uses against us, going to continue to blind us?

As I progress through the rest of this book, I'd like you to pause for a second. If you haven't already by now, I am asking you to take a retrospective look at your life and seek to pinpoint those choices that have brought you to your current state of existence. Don't look retrospectively from a place of remorse or regret because our God is sovereign and daily unfolds great organization and beauty out of many a chaotic lives. Look more so from the perspective of acute awareness.

More importantly, I want you to take a deep introspective look at yourself. As you read, I implore you to observe and make careful note of these key points:

a. "For I know the plans I have for you said the Lord…" Observe God's guidance on my life, especially in areas I had no opportunity to control. (See Jeremiah 29:11.)

b. Observe my decision making and the results they generated due to the training I received on navigating the roadmap as a firstborn son. (See Proverbs 22:6.)

c. Observe the impressions I have been fortunate and blessed to leave on lives which have depended on me for guidance as a result of the roadmap.

d. Personalize the stories and insert yourself or your son and ask or visualize how you or he would have responded in a similar position. If a change is needed, evaluate and implement a change.

e. Evaluate how you want your firstborn son (infant or teenager) to impact his society in the future. Make a commitment to train them to navigate since you can't guide them. A trained person is always capable of revisiting the fundamentals of the training when mistakes befall them.

CHAPTER EIGHT:

Responsibility and Preference Come with the Position

In Debt to a People I Have Never Known

We have been speaking of the responsibility that comes with the position in the sense of decision making we are confronted with, generally in the present. What about those responsibilities we are told belong to us in the sense of future responsibilities?

I was born in Liberia, West Africa, to a mother and father that are Cameroonians by birth (in Central Africa). They left their native land as a very young couple to pursue a life and career in a foreign land. They raised their children to understand that there is a larger family that exists in Cameroon. I traveled to Cameroon once for vacation at the age of five.

Our parents earned measly missionary/teacher salaries and only traveled back momentarily for funerals and other very important issues. They could not afford to take us home as a family frequently. As such, I know very little of my blood (Cameroonian) heritage. However, my parents have continuously called me to the task of attending to the Bambolo legacy, claiming responsibility for the extended family that resides in Cameroon. In short, I feel as if in debt to a people I have never known or have never known me.

This is a tough responsibility for me to own. Not much in life gets done until we accept or take ownership of the task at hand. First and foremost, I have my family to sustain and nurture now as a husband and father—not an easy task. Secondly, the task definitely carries more the desires of my parents than it does mine. My parents have seen me accomplish the mission and responsibility they first set before me of restoring the family following the loss of war. As such, their confidence in making such a request of me is strong. Yet and still, I seek to reconcile their request with the battles of adequately providing for my immediate family. How do I make such a decision?

The problem is not about refusing to honor my parents' request. Know them or not, the relatives in Cameroon are part of my family and more importantly God's family. I cannot jump to claim I love God with my heroic actions on mission projects and the sorts without first obeying His command for my family and home. The Lord does give specific instruction to this matter in His Scripture.

"Give the people these instructions, too, so that no one may be open to blame. If anyone does not provide for his relatives, and especially for his immediate family, he has denied the faith and is worse than an unbeliever" (1 Tim. 5:7-8).

As stated clearly, it is part of God's law, which I have chosen to know and honor. There is also more on God's law when it comes to honoring my family.

"Therefore a man shall leave his father and his mother and shall become united and cleave to his wife, and they shall become one flesh" (Gen. 2:24, italics mine, AMP).

It seems to me that both of these verses stress the importance of my responsibility to family. However there is a greater level of responsibility expected from me toward my immediate family, beginning with my wife. For the cause of marriage and the responsibility to my wife and children, the request of my parents takes a secondary position. Some will probably dare to argue that Ephesians 6 speaks of children honoring their parents, the first commandment with promise, and the fifth out of the Ten Commandments. In making such a decision, I have to employ my biblical order of priority here first and foremost.

What is my order of priority?

- It begins with the command for me to love my God with all my heart, soul, and mind. The first order of business is to know God thoroughly. Firstborn son, you will find that this command is just as important when it comes to being the father and man God has required us to be.

- Ephesians 5 speaks of the requirement to love my wife as Christ loved the church. Christ loved the church sacrificially enough to give His life for her, His bride.

- Ephesians 6:4 and Colossians 3:21 instruct that I am not to embitter or exasperate my children as a father. I have to ensure they are raised in an environment that allows them to pursue God healthily.

- My extended family and relatives are also important as stated in 1 Timothy 5:8.

- The final priority on this list is my work. God created man for a personal relationship with Him. But Genesis 2:15, before the sin and fall of Adam, says that God put man into the Garden of Eden to work and take care of it. We were also created to honor God with our work.

These are the priorities that govern the most important and critical decisions of my life.

In making such decisions, my first and most important act is to spend time in prayer and petition to God. After that, I discuss the situation with my wife in order to determine our thoughts on the subject, as well as the effects that it will have on our family. Until we can determine that we are suitably capable of sustaining the mental, physical, and spiritual health of our marriage and home we are not going to commit to such responsibility. It is only out of the overflow of matters that affect the immediate family will we take on the requirements of extended relatives as requested by my parents.

Firstborn son, married or not, this is the order of priority with which we are to pursue our decisions in life. If you are not married, I am aware there won't be a wife to consult. The order of priority is still one that you must align yourself with. God and the knowledge of His Word available to you never change, so dive in deep and seek understanding. Discuss with your son or your children, or at least consider the impact on their lives with more gravity (as God's command), than you have ever done before. Consider the effect your decision will have on other family members, especially those directly dependent on you for sustenance. Additionally, how will the decision you are making impact your ability to perform work that honors your God and in most cases provides the stability your family needs. Independently wealthy or not, what are you doing that fulfills God's command in Genesis 2:15? All other considerations have to come after you have addressed these priorities.

Is this something I can discuss with those who speak into my life influentially or my accountability partners to get objective and biblical feedback in case I am missing something? It is indeed. This is one of the reasons why it is important to surround myself with a solid and respected group of individuals, primarily men that I deeply trust to give me a direct and spiritually honest criticism. Influential individuals are simply people that I admire (men such as pastors, my father, and successful leaders) because they have and continue to travel the narrow and godly road I now navigate. And I have the ability to interact with them directly. My accountability partners are a group of men (generally no more than four) that have agreed to confide in each other for life's most intimate challenges and successes. In essence there is a bond practically governed by an oath or vow of honesty to each other. It is an intimate and confidential relationship and brotherhood.

Early on in my life I did not pursue my decisions with this structure in place. Although I had an excellent helper (my wife) that my heavenly Father had provided me, I failed to realize how incredible God's design is for my life. *God blesses what He has installed.* Comparing the outcomes of my decisions now to my past is a no contest. They are much more fruitful if aligned with the order of priority. I am not saying I no longer make errors in my decisions. The fact of the matter is, even the wrong decisions are not as destructive to our family because we are all (wife and children) on board and are prepared to collectively make the necessary sacrifice to rectify the situation. Firstborn son, that is what managing your family entails as is described in 1 Timothy 3:4-5.

CHAPTER NINE:

Firstborn Son, the Coach, Mentor, and Friend

As firstborn sons we are designed by our God to fill positions of leadership, authority, and accept that others are clearly dependent on us. I wrote earlier that the position of firstborn son sometimes feels like a curse, a gift, or a passion. I have to say that the subject matter we are about to discuss definitely fills the passion aspect. It is a calling.

"For this very reason, make every effort to add to your faith goodness; and to goodness, knowledge; and to knowledge, self-control; and to self-control, perseverance; and to perseverance, godliness; and to godliness, brotherly kindness; and to brotherly kindness, love. For if you possess these qualities in increasing measure, they will keep you from being ineffective and unproductive in your knowledge of our Lord Jesus Christ. But if anyone does not have them, he is nearsighted and blind, and has forgotten that he has been cleansed from his past sins. Therefore, my brothers, be all the more eager to make your calling and election sure. For if you do these things, you will never fall, and you will receive a rich welcome into the eternal kingdom of our Lord and Savior Jesus Christ" (2 Pet. 1:5-11).

"With this in mind, we constantly pray for you, that our God may count you worthy of his calling, and that by his power he may fulfill every good purpose of yours and every act prompted by your faith" (2 Thess. 1:11).

There is nothing grander than the fulfillment that comes from attending to someone's needs successfully. Whether friends, family, or otherwise, the passion drives me to seek to enable them to avoid being nearsighted and blinded by their sins. I don't know of a single soul that is not thrilled when they realize the results of their productivity. God has put us (firstborn sons) in a phenomenal position to grow in our life's journey with a special zeal to positively impact the lives of the people around us regularly.

As you read the verses of 2 Peter 1:5-11, be very committed. Seek to add to your life the qualities that render you effective and productive. However, do so in the knowledge of our Lord and Savior Jesus Christ, the source of your effectiveness and productivity. In doing these things, not only will you be welcomed into the eternal kingdom but the Scripture says it will be a "rich welcome." Remember the description of the various other religions, cults, occults, and conspiracy theorists, as opposed to true Christianity? There are a couple of very distinctive qualities that differentiate the two sides. The collective group of cults and so on is more concerned with personal self-help development and satisfaction. True Christianity and the Holy Scriptures urges believers to exercise our faith in service toward and for the development of others. This verse clearly confirms just that and assures you what our God expects of us. Look at the list of these qualities we are to practice. See if you can find any that are self-promoting as opposed to other centered. The evidence of these characteristics can only be displayed by our acts of service toward others. The qualities listed are:

- Goodness

- Knowledge

- Self-Control

- Perseverance

- Godliness

- Brotherly kindness

- Love

How many of these can you exemplify or perfect in increasing measure without application toward someone else? None of these can be perfected in that selfish or self-promoting manner.

My Group of Influential Individuals or Circle of Influence

A person's circle of influence is extremely important for the outcome they desire to achieve or help others achieve. I am sure you have heard the statement, "You are who you associate with." Firstborn son, have you looked at who you associate with lately? Are you wondering why you can't seem to live a victorious life or win? Are you wondering why you feel powerless and consistently failing with your wife and children? Are you wondering why you always seem at risk of being in trouble with the law or authority figures? Look around you and assess who you associate with. There is a good chance those elements contribute to your failures.

As a successful person in general, but more importantly in this case, as a coach, mentor, or influential friend whom others depend on, I have to first shape my circle of influence. Those influential sources which engulf me cannot be different from or sub par in comparison to who I desire to be. As a matter of fact, I have to set the bar so high that I sometimes feel it is impossible to attain. That way I never complacently feel I have arrived. I have to consistently work on my circle of influence desiring measurable increase in every area. The people that I seek to emulate in my life are consistently doing great things and thereby push me to do the same or better. It is not a bad idea at this moment to revisit the qualities listed above that allow our calling or passion to experience effectiveness and productivity.

The Bible verse 2 Peter 1:8 (above) addresses being effective and productive in the "knowledge of our Lord Jesus Christ." Why is the knowledge of our Lord Jesus Christ so important? Why is it important to know what He says in His Scripture, "I am the vine you are the branches?" (See John 15:5.) In other words, stay connected to Jesus as your source of life. Why is it important to know He instructs us to bear fruit? Why is it important to know that the Scriptures describe evidence of the Holy Spirit in our lives as fruit (fruit of the Spirit)? *It is because the purpose (the calling or passion) of our lives, which requires "knowledge of our Lord Jesus Christ," is evidenced in effectiveness and productivity (fruit).* Our Lord Jesus Christ is all about productivity generated by Him, through Him, and for Him.

It was famed scholar Joseph Barber Lightfoot who provided us the quote, "There is no persuasiveness more effectual than the transparency of a single heart, of a sincere life."[21]

As such, allow me to be transparent. I have for a while now known my calling and passion is coaching, mentoring, and teaching. I have pursued that calling in what represented to me at the time "extra-curricular activities" as a high school basketball coach, small group facilitator, firstborn son, and so forth. However, I have not yet pursued such an occupation with a full-time commitment. That is partially due to a commitment made to my wife during our efforts to restore our marriage and relationship. I have held multiple successful positions in the world of corporate America as a communications consultant. But I have no desire to climb the ladder to become a C-level executive. I have won multiple awards and held leadership roles on high-producing teams.

I find it extremely difficult to justify the productivity gain from signing a corporate contract of any kind as more valid than the alignment or redirection of a young impressionable life, or any life for that matter. The latter to me is the fruit Christ desires. As a result, I have continuously asked myself, "What am I doing here if I do not clearly see a career path or my life's work?" I do not say this to belittle the corporate world and its greatness, especially since it has fed my family for many years and does continue its provisions. I say it mainly to be transparent concerning a calling on my life that I have not answered fully possibly until now.

So, if that is the case, who am I allowing to impact me as influential sources? The people that are allowed to pour into me the qualities of goodness, knowledge, self-control, perseverance, godliness, brotherly-kindness, and love have to be an extremely selective group. Those people have to live increasingly immeasurable human life since that is what I am instructed to achieve. They are always striving to improve and show no complacency in their passion for Jesus Christ. And because Christ demands effectiveness and productivity via the knowledge of who He is, they are always producing fruit. In the true sense of the words, coaching, mentoring, and friendship are all about fruitful relationships thereby producing fruit. In pursuing this I must have a productive circle of influence to teach me or from which to draw.

Allow me to introduce a man that has impacted me greatly as a source of influence far greater than money ever could. He is Dr. Kenneth "Hutch" Hutcherson. I have many great men and friends in my sphere, but God has used Hutch the greatest on me. He has been a great brother and friend.

> "Brothers, I could not address you as spiritual but as worldly—mere infants in Christ. I gave you milk, not solid food, for you were not yet ready for it. Indeed, you are still not ready. You are still worldly. For since there is jealousy and quarreling among you, are you not worldly? Are you not acting like mere men?" (1 Cor. 3:1-3).

> "But when he asks, he must believe and not doubt, because he who doubts is like a wave of the sea, blown and tossed by the wind. That man should not think he will receive anything from the Lord; he is a double-minded man, unstable in all he does" (James 1:6-8).

The above Scriptures describe to the fullest the worldly man that I was when Hutch came into my life. I had grown up in the church and had done so many wonderful things throughout my upbringing. The singing, youth ministry, Sunday school teaching, and serving were all part of my life. Sadly however, I did all of those things without any substance to my offering, definitely not giving God my first fruits. I did them all as a "milk-drinking," immature Christian. That culture of religion (or being religious without substance) in the context of the Christian is so prevalent around the world and in America. In my upbringing, especially in Liberia, I very frequently saw and heard of men who called themselves pastors, preachers, and shepherds of God's flock. Unfortunately the whole community knew that they were not above reproach, nor did they try to pursue that requirement. The biggest known sin of the clergy in my upbringing was men being unfaithful to their wives.

Before I met Hutch, the Bible did not speak to me as it does now. I remember making this unbelievably inconsiderate, arrogant, and selfish statement to my wife when she asked that we go to church more consistently. I said, "I know what the church is all about. I am not ready to go yet. When I am ready, I will know because it will be time to cut every sinful thing [night clubbing, drinking, filthy language, and so on] out of my life. When I do it, I'll do it 100 percent." Someone may look at that statement and see nothing wrong with such an honest and clean observation or intention. Yeah, if you are a milk-drinking Christian, then sure nothing is wrong.

A person who truly understands Scripture on the other hand says, "Now that is and arrogant and selfish person." First and foremost, that statement portrayed that my Christianity was all about me and when it was convenient for me. I clearly did not know much of anything of what church was about as I claimed. (Even now I still have a whole lot to learn.) I had failed my wife on the biblical mandate that God has set for me as her husband and the high priest of my home. But more importantly, what if Christ had the same attitude of neglect and told God He wasn't ready to die for the my sins, although He knew the importance of the blood sacrifice? Where would I be? My views on Christianity were all backward.

When I actually got the chance to sit before Hutch and talk one-on-one, it was because my wife had finally had enough, after pleading with me for years, or my selfishness and arrogance. In the trawl of divorce, my wife had moved out of our home and was living with a friend as we sought to finalize legal separation. For all it is worth, the great reasons for which we pursued the marital union meant nothing compared to my selfishness. In the art of renaming sin, I abused my wife's rightful place for the so-called nobility of family fortune and financial gain. And I could not understand why she couldn't see that my actions were for our benefit. I went seeking help from the only place I knew how—the church. And even then, when Hutch began to show me the errors of my ways that landed me in this position, arrogance brewed within me. How dare another man tell me how to run my home and marriage?

The lovely thing is that he didn't telling me what to do. Through his keen knowledge and gifted understanding of Scripture, he showed me how to embrace life with Christ. He showed me how to study the Scriptures intimately, apply them, and watch them produce fruit effectively. It has been over eight years now that I continue to sit in a discipleship setting once a week with an intimate brotherhood of over twenty men led by Hutch.

In that time, I have watched Hutch live the Scriptures uncompromisingly literally for the world to see. While other pastors are content to live inside the four walls of their comfortable churches and allow biblical values to be politicized and eroded, I have seen this man stand up and hold firm to the unchanging Word of God. I have seen his vision for proof of no-charge or free adoptions take up root against the big business that it is. I have seen the life of my friend and brother effectively producing lives and soldiers for God's kingdom repeatedly.

Regardless of all those wonderful accolades mentioned above, nothing of Hutch's has impacted and influenced me more as his life in the last couple of years. I have watched my brother go through a harsh and severe bout with cancer and display truly unwavering faith. He is very much aware to what extent the possible outcomes exist, including death. No man faces those possibilities without the thoughts. However, his countenance stays strong. He made a profound statement that has impacted my life forever. For those of us who have intimate dealings and understand the man that he is, as well as his passion for the Scriptures, we say "Wow!" He once said, "You've watched me live for Christ. If that is where the cancer takes me, I'll show you how to die for

Christ." With Christ indeed *all* things are possible. I can't wait to see the new and renewed Hutch as he beats this cancer.

That is a view into the circle of influence that engulfs me. What is yours, firstborn son?

Circle of Influence I Created for My Dependents

A second circle of influence, and somewhat more important, is the influence I create or offer to those who look up to me. I must create a positive sphere of influence for my players, mentees, and my friends. What social examples do I provide for them to follow? The saying goes, "actions speak louder than words." The same principles and qualities for effectiveness and productivity as described in 2 Peter 1:5-11 apply here as well. The only difference here is that I am picking personalities to whom I will give the authority to impact others (sometimes incapable of defending themselves). "Others" in this case, are people who have confided their utmost trust in me to protect them in their most vulnerable moments. Trust requires them to let down all barriers of protection they may have constructed. Therefore, the structural integrity of this sphere of influence must be even more secure.

In my experience as an athletic coach, it is somewhat impossible to accurately pick characters that perfectly execute on the tasks of teaching and mentoring exactly as I do. Second Peter 1:5-11 definitely draws out a good job description for me to utilize in the selection process. However, I must continually test the structure of the sphere by frequently dialoguing with those in charge. I must make sure to maintain a safe haven. I must also be realistic that I won't win every kid, and I can only win the ones that allow us to speak into their hearts.

Allow me then to describe a few areas where God has used me, and I don't expect Him stop anytime soon.

Firstborn Son, the Coach

I spent six years as a basketball coach at a local high school. I have spent numerous years with kids, especially teenage young men in and around the profession. My wife is also a high school volleyball coach and that also leads to frequent interaction with young athletes. I specifically love the area of the elementary to the high school levels because I feel there is a great opportunity to plant some significant seeds in the impressionable young minds of these individuals. There is always great opportunity to impart knowledge in a mentoring fashion to individuals at any stage of life. As our Lord does, we are to be prepared in and out of season to meet people where they are and present them what they require. The teenage years just seem to be the most fertile ground to offer a roadmap. Here are a few of stories from my experience.

Authority Was Not His Thing

I am going to call this young man Barkley. Barkley is not a firstborn son. As a matter of fact he is smack in the middle of a pack with older siblings and younger siblings. I can list multiple occasions when Barkley and I did not see eye to eye. I had to suspend him from the team several times. Many times I had both teammates and coaches asking that we just let him go. No one was safe from a good confrontation with Barkley. It didn't matter whether it was at practice, summer workouts, spring or summer league games, or actual regular season games; he had no regard for authority. He had pretty much raised himself and had to fight to get any attention since mom and dad, divorced, were not around to give it to him. I believe Barkley's problem with authority resurrected from anger at feeling lonely and deserted although he existed in what was a crowd of a family. He felt, "If no adult cares about me, I won't care about them either."

I remember a conversation I had with Barkley. He had a girlfriend that was a year or so older than him. He loved her intensely. Once he came to practice deeply distraught and unable to focus. As a matter of fact, he came in late, which was greatly unacceptable in our program. He had a somber look on his face, so I asked him what was wrong. His girlfriend was away at college and happened to get friendly with a few friends of the opposite sex, which threatened their relationship. He was afraid she may have made a terrible mistake or was going to make one to jeopardize their relationship and future together.

I asked him a simple question, "Why do you expect her to hold the bar extremely high when you haven't led her with such examples? You haven't held the bar high." When Barkley was messing around with her, kissing, petting, cuddling, creating circumstances with the potential of having sex he did not realize that he was setting her up for failure by lowering the standards he expected of her. Now that she was away and exploring with others as she had done with him, he was distraught. That seemed to turn the light on in his mind and settle him down. He wasn't happy to hear that, but it was the truth. He could not simply sit by and point the finger at how horrible a person she was being to him; he had to now accept a share of the responsibility for her fall. Barkley is a good kid and does not hesitate to own up to consequences good or bad, I must say. He did just that in this case.

Firstborn son, are you owning up to the mistakes of those dependent on you, your wife, children, and friends, and assessing how you may have led them into those errors before you boil up in anger and beat them down verbally, or sadly, physically in some cases?

Barkley is loyal, an extremely hard worker, a pretty good student, and easily had the most 'can't lose' attitude on the team. He frequently led the drills and took even those moments as a challenge. Barkley has chosen a career path that will probably baffle many, but it did not surprise me a bit. He has chosen a career path that requires some of the greatest intestinal fortitude and discipline this world demands. Furthermore, for a person who supposedly was uncontrollable, with administrators considering expelling him from school multiple times, he has chosen a career path that demands absolute submission to authority. He is about the youngest of his class but is proving to be among the top prospects for success in training regiment that usually sees 80 to 90 percent attrition of the initial class size.

I will be honest that I didn't know how much I had reached Barkley until I received a call from him this summer. He was calling to fill me in on his progress. His words shocked me. He said, "I want to thank you for all you did for me. I thank you for being the one consistent man in my life. No matter what happened between us, I always knew you would be there for me."

Barkley knows that I will forever be here for him as long as God keeps me on this Earth. Firstborn son, there are many times that you will feel you are not reaching your son or children. Do not stop working. Do not stop trying. Sometimes you are sowing a field that you will harvest and get to see your children respond to. Sometimes you are sowing a field that someone else may harvest if your children respond very late in life. All that matters is that they respond. Remember this comment also, "A farmer never sows and reaps in the same season." The statement is a great depiction for having faith that God does answer our prayers. In many cases, He simply answers us in a different season than we want or expect. This manner of response is God's design to keep us focusing on the "giver" rather than the gift.

Reshaping His View...

I want to tell you about another young man I will call Jericho. Jericho's life in our program is a true example of what can happen when a village raises a child. There is no way that one person could have accomplished this task. There were many people involved at various levels of maturity that had a significant hand in shaping the clay that he was into what he has become.

When Jericho came to our program he was a slightly overweight kid who had lost his father in a seriously life-scarring scenario. He had decided to absolutely reject school, he had no regard for authority or loyalty toward friends, and last but not least, he rejected his family, especially his mother. Academically, Jericho could not maintain classroom focus long enough to secure even an F in special education level classes. His way of shielding himself from people who would eventually notice his flaws was by a clever ploy of disruptive behavior. In a weird way, the disruptive behavior took the focus away from his flaws but nevertheless kept him as the center of attention, especially amongst his peers. Although nothing else seemed to provide a safe place of consistent interest for Jericho, the lure of basketball seemed his only hope. Basketball was the only activity that appeared to hold his attention.

Although basketball was taking a role of first love with Jericho, his rejection of authority still posed a major obstacle. He was also practically prevented from participating in any activity because he didn't have the ability to achieve academic upkeep. In a variety of instances, I had parents and players demanding that Jericho be ushered out of the program due to his disruptive nature. It was extremely difficult to not oblige. However, God was and is writing a tremendous story although we all felt a tremendous burden to break him into submission.

I am glad God had me where He did for that season of life. I had a tremendous number of talks with Jericho, sometimes urging his obedience and many times threatening him with other consequences. I mentioned earlier there is a great responsibility on our shoulders concerning the people that we allow around our sons and dependents with regard to their sphere of influence. In comes the perfect all-American family.

Jericho needed something greater by far than basketball could give him. To convince himself of where his life was headed, he needed a full frontal example of a true and complete family. Many young and confused men in this country like Jericho need an honest example of a solid and healthy family structure—not necessarily NBA stars, football stars, movie stars, and the likes. The odds of them achieving stardom and fame are slim to none and usually leave a huge feeling of failure and disappointment. The odds of these young men having a family of their own are most likely and warrant the most preparation. However, those of us who have the examples they need seem to shun them out of fear that they will influence and do more damage to our families and our children than we can possibly do to impact their fragile lives. As a result, rather than embrace them and put them on the right track, we threaten our children with punishment for even talking to them. Have we no confidence we have trained our children well enough?

In Jericho's case, I was lucky to have picked as part of my staff and sphere of influence the perfect family for him. They had a son close to his age who was also a basketball star in our program. More importantly, he was brought into a home where chores and celebrations, as well as anger and happiness existed. Conversely, none of these eroded the eternal joy and unity of the family. He did learn to trust and understand the dynamics of a loving father and mother, and the little siblings that existed within this family unit. He was loved as one of their own.

I can't tell you how amazing a story God is writing in this young man, how incredible a restoration story he is. God graced me with an opportunity to reflect on his progress. I sat in a coffee shop once and a young man walked by that was the absolute image of the old Jericho—untamed dreadlocks, hiding behind a heavy coat in the middle of summer season, and sagging pants. He looked so much like Jericho in stature, with headphones on his head that screamed, "Do not dare talk to me." Less than five minutes later, while my mind still lingered on what would have become of Jericho, Jericho walked by not knowing I was in the area and watching him. He was very clean, shorts with a polo shirt tucked in, a very confident and engaging posture, well-groomed dreadlocks, and a seemingly focused attitude as he was heading to work. This was a person no one would have considered giving a job to just a few years before, and he would have gladly hid behind that excuse.

There is a comment that sticks with me to this day that came from Jericho. It was his senior year in high school. We both knew he was not going to graduate like the rest of his mates since he was so far behind. He had committed to his academics and had been working extremely hard the last year and a half to two. A phenomenal athlete that many college coaches desired, but he didn't have the academics to qualify. He knew all of this and could easily drum up an excuse to quit. Instead these were the words uttered, "Coach, at this point I don't care if I don't make it to the NBA. I just want to study hard and get my degree."

I just spoke to Jericho yesterday. A few years removed from that statement, he was all smiles through the phone, studying hard, and enjoying the blessings of basketball as a successful student athlete. What a blessing!

Firstborn son, what sphere of influence have you created for those dependent on you?

Some You Pray and Wait for Like the Father of the Prodigal Son

Not every story ends up warm and fuzzy. Sometimes you see so much of yourself in a person, and you think, "I can absolutely reach this one," but you can't, even with the purest of hearts because God has not designed you for the harvest. So it was with a young man I choose to call Dimitri.

Dimitri came into my life as an extremely high profile personality. Even then, with all of the negatives that surrounded him, he still had the world of professional athletics at his fingertips. Much like my own, his world as a firstborn son was laced with expectations that far outreached and outpaced his ability to fully comprehend at a young age. It is extremely tough when fathers see a thoroughbred with unquestionable and unimaginable upside within their possession. The father has this phenom that is his own flesh and blood, but the father does not have the tools to maximize the potential. I tried to come beside Dimitri as a trusted confidant with a desire to help him understand his surroundings with conversations, books, and other materials. We had some good conversations, but I was eventually asked by his father to refrain from such influences. Dimitri had been taught that everyone who surrounded him was out to get something from him and abuse his fortune. As a result, I could not reach father or son intimately for a great long while, especially while they were in my immediate daily circle of existence. I have many thoughts of what the relationship could have been if Dimitri and I had truly connected.

He went on to live the high profile life with many a public bumps and bruises along the way. He seemed to have landed in a place that embraced him, and it seems he embraced in return. In recent years and months, the true person he is has begun to emerge. His public image continues to echo more of his successes and leadership talent as a firstborn son than he realizes. He is starting to welcome more of the responsibilities he rejected for so long, that others are beginning to comment on how selfless a person he has become. These are traits that I noticed in our many conversations even in the midst of confrontations we would have. He has never been a rude or arrogant person to me. As a matter of fact, he was deeply soft spoken and accepting of constructive criticism. But he had been taught to air a different persona in public, one of gruff toughness and arrogance. As a result, he greatly lacked the social skills for deep trusting friendships.

It was extremely difficult to see and observe that the road he traveled was bound for headaches and pain. I mentioned to him several times that in my desire to mentor him he got away with things that others would not tolerate and that those behaviors would cost him dearly. They did. It was even harder to leave him with the following statement, but I did. I told him, "I have no desire to force myself to be a part of your life. But always remember, I will always be here for you no matter what. Just call me when you need me." I maintain that vow to this day and will do so for as long as I live. There have been a few times that he has come by my home unannounced or made a phone call to me out of the blue, so I know he remembers our talk. I have made attempts to visit with him as well so that he realizes my commitment still stands.

There is no giving up on any of my players, much like I will never give up on my children, my own flesh and blood. Like the father of the prodigal son, I wait, looking at the road I expect him to take when he returns.

"The Parable of the Lost Son
Jesus continued: 'There was a man who had two sons. The younger one said to his father, "Father, give me my share of the estate." So he divided his property between them.

Not long after that, the younger son got together all he had, set off for a distant country and there squandered his wealth in wild living. After he had spent everything, there was a severe famine in that whole country, and he began to be in need. So he went and hired himself out to a citizen of that country, who sent him to his fields to feed pigs. He longed to fill his stomach with the pods that the pigs were eating, but no one gave him anything.

When he came to his senses, he said, "How many of my father's hired men have food to spare, and here I am starving to death! I will set out and go back to my father and say to him: Father, I have sinned against heaven and against you. I am no longer worthy to be called your son; make me like one of your hired men." So he got up and went to his father.

But while he was still a long way off, his father saw him and was filled with compassion for him; he ran to his son, threw his arms around him and kissed him.

The son said to him, "Father, I have sinned against heaven and against you. I am no longer worthy to be called your son." But the father said to his servants, "Quick! Bring the best robe and put it on him. Put a ring on his finger and sandals on his feet. Bring the fattened calf and kill it. Let's have a feast and celebrate. For this son of mine was dead and is alive again; he was lost and is found." So they began to celebrate" (Luke 15:11-24, italics mine).

Firstborn Son, the Mentor and Friend

Not too long ago, through the world of social media, I ran across a good friend whom I hadn't seen or spoken to in many years. I remembered her as a feisty and fun-loving person. She had since gone on to marry her high school sweetheart and had a beautiful family as evidence. As we communicated, I sensed there was something not so feisty about her and that she was not the personality I remembered. She then informed me she was in the process of getting a divorce.

Marriage is an area where God has done a miraculous work on my wife and me. Our journey deeply convicts us into believing every destroyed marriage is salvageable, if the hearts involved desire true and obedient godly restoration. My wife and I frequently find that God drops struggling couples into our laps, and we have accepted the responsibility.

In this case, we invited the family to take a trip into town and spend a weekend with us. The weekend also happened to be Fourth of July. *There is no better way to convict a person who desires to believe but can't find the courage to, than to have them walk in the reality of their fear.* We talked to them for a few days and described the restoration that occurred with our marriage from the dumps that we found ourselves in about nine years ago. They were in a very similar place.

In about a four-day period, they got to see a great deal of how we lived as a family and couple who had walked the exact road they were now walking. They got to see that the restoration was real and that a true partnership had ensued, especially in how we raise our children. They were in our most intimate space for more than eighty hours straight. I have to say their courage was amazing in order to take this trip. Our initial conversation had been less than a week earlier. The weekend that they spent with us was the weekend they had chosen for her to move out with the kids with no intent of returning.

However, I write about this young couple because the greatest take away for them that weekend was seeing how hard we work as a couple to shape our circle of influence, as well as the one we create for our children. They saw and understood that those choices are deliberate on our part. We commit to activities that are absolutely designed to edify our spiritual growth, marital relationship, and family unity. Christ is always at the helm of this vessel, and that is not just a wish. It is a reality and truth.

I believe the most revealing thing to them was seeing the actual Fourth of July gathering we attended that weekend. They were definitely strangers in the midst of the crowd but in a really good way. There are many couples and children that make up our intimate social circle. *All of us are absolute Bible-believing Christians seeking to fit in God's world, not trying to make Him fit in ours.* The values we seek to bestow on our children are shared by those we associate with so that our children are not confused. Men were being aggressive and playing sports in true godly harmony, yet fully aware that they are fathers and husbands first. Women were being loving mothers and socializing verbally, making sure the kids (husbands included) were being fed and also engaging in some sports activities. Fathers were water sliding with the children into the pool. Mothers were taking kids for rides on four-wheelers.

My point is, regardless of the size of the crowd and the kinds of activities, the couple saw that this kind of healthy environment for all in the family unit is possible, and the restoration and nurturing of the marital relationship has to be by design. They had to begin to discuss how they were to create a similar and trusting environment for their family, an environment where men and women jump to unintimidating and accountable relationships. The circle of influence cannot be left to chance.

These are just a few of the many stories I could write about in my role as coach, mentor, and friend. There are adult and parent stories around coaching as well that I have been fortunate to learn a great deal from. And surely as you can see, I am far from perfect in the performance of my role and duties, which I pray about. But I also pray to God everyday that I am perfect in my availability for His work. The passion is what drives me to stand tall as a first-born son and say in speech, written words, or actions, "Let me walk beside you on this journey."

Ultimately God is the designer of the masterpiece He wants to create on the canvas of you and me.

CHAPTER TEN:

*Heart to Heart, One on One, Behind Closed Doors,
Let's Talk Privately*

As you read this book, I am sure it is quite apparent to you by now that I am fully aware of and accept God the Father's calling on my life. I have no doubt that He has been deeply involved in every single moment and every activity I have been engaged in. As you read my life's stories, my hope was to bring you along in every one of these events. Similarly as happens when I tell of these occurrences in person, I have no doubt you had moments of anxiety and suspense as if you were there right beside me in the midst of war. You might have even felt incredibly angered at many of the mistreatment and discriminating circumstances that occurred as well.

Call my life what you like, extreme, traumatic, and/or any other description that fits. But think of this, God did not make an error in building and molding me the way He did. Sure, there are a lot of incidents that I would describe as unfortunate just as quickly as you would. The fact of the matter is I may not be in the position that I am now if He hadn't been as specific as He was in creating these incredible circumstances. Just the same however, I submit that He hasn't made any error in molding you the way He has either. The call of God on your life is no less important because you didn't encounter the kind of so-called extreme or traumatic experiences I did. As a matter of fact, you may have encountered situations much worse than mine.

The fact that you are reading this book, or are alive and cognizant enough to do so, is truly an expression of God's sovereignty. Many have lost their lives or lost the ability to think and reason and are now mentally challenged, something that so many of us take for granted, as a result of acts and occurrences far less threatening. Some people you and I know or have heard of simply went to sleep and did not awake; they died in their sleep. Are we any better, or do we deserve any better than they do? I doubt that.

The impact this book is having on you at this moment as you have continued to read is more than enough proof that God has a tug on your heart and expects an action out of you. If it isn't so, I do not believe this book would have had as much of a draw to you. God expects you to make a stand and take action in making a change to a matter that He has prepared you to be sympathetic to. This is the profound nature or manner by which God calls each of us to an action He has prepared us for long in advance. Every passionate soul, especially Christian believers with incredibly positive impacting ministries in our society and world, are drawn to action by the great story and influence of another. The ultimate Great Story happens to be none other than Jesus Christ. His life has called countless people to action. Some are motivated in support of His life, but sadly many are in opposition to the nature and person He is. So, what action are you going to take in response to God's calling on your life? What is your call to action?

Firstborn son, our society and culture is content with us being passive in responding to our responsibilities. It plays right into the hands of the culture and worldly, as opposed to godly, desires if we are reactive rather than proactive. With the development and upbringing you have received, God has put you in this blessed role, firstborn son, to rise to the occasion and do something great. He has designed you to overachieve on the responsibility He has given you. Take the challenge and go on the offensive rather than defensive response when it comes to saving or redeeming our family, home, culture, and society. As a very good friend describes, we are "the men at the city gate." We ward off and defend against anything that threatens and seeks to destroy our society. The *men at the city gate* signify stability for our communities and society. The *men at the city gate* observe and know everyone that belongs within and those that don't. The *men at the city gate* are prepared to confront those elements that threaten to destroy us and do not belong within our walls. Because the *men at the city gate* rise to the occasion righteously, our society finds godly peace and rest.

"FIRST OF all, then, I admonish and urge that petitions, prayers, intercessions, and thanksgivings be offered on behalf of all men, For kings and all who are in positions of authority or high responsibility, that [outwardly] we may pass a quiet and undisturbed life [and inwardly] a peaceable one in all godliness and reverence and seriousness in every way. For such [praying] is good and right, and [it is] pleasing and acceptable to God our Savior, Who wishes all men to be saved and [increasingly] to perceive and recognize and discern and know precisely and correctly the [divine] Truth" (1 Tim. 2:1-4, AMP).

What about you who are reading this book? As you read this book, where is God calling you and has specifically designed you to stand righteously? I have a feeling you know quite well where He has called you, but you have disobeyed His request on your life to stand for Him. When it comes to God's magnificent creation, nothing is insignificant. A word to the wise, don't think a call to stand in your home and family is any less important to God than some world-renowned multi-continental evangelical ministry. He has a strange way of demonstrating His miracles to us when we make ourselves FAT (Faithful, Available, and Teachable).

Lavish and the Humanly Illogical Blessing

Speaking of taking a stand in our homes and for our families, I want to elaborate on a subject that is near and dear to my heart as one who frequently engages youth. You may recall this statistical line in chapter 1 of this book.

"In 2008, 75 percent of White, non-Hispanic, 64 percent of Hispanic, and 35 percent of Black children lived with two married parents."[22]

Firstborn son, are you a part of this statistic or on your way to add to the trend? Stand up and fix the situation. You have probably heard or said the statement, "Nothing is impossible with God." As a matter of fact, when it comes to God, *IMPOSSIBLE* truly reads as I – M – POSSIBLE (I am possible). Many of us pray and ask God to perform a miracle in our lives. Then we sit around waiting for God to give us hard evidence of how He is going to do the miraculous rather than step out by faith. By the way, if God shows you the evidence that you seek on your terms, then it is no longer "a miracle." Miracles are meant to astonish us. What you have evidence of prior to its occurrence can no longer astonish you. Listen to how God desires to fill us who hunger and thirst for His miracles.

"For my thoughts are not your thoughts,
neither are your ways my ways," declares the LORD.
As the heavens are higher than the earth, so are my ways higher than your ways
and my thoughts than your thoughts.
As the rain and the snow come down from heaven,
and do not return to it without watering the earth
and making it bud and flourish, so that it yields seed for the sower and bread for the eater,
so is my word that goes out from my mouth: It will not return to me empty,
but will accomplish what I desire and achieve the purpose for which I sent it" (Isa. 55:8-11).

The Childstats.gov statistics listed above amaze me on all fronts about all the races but none more than the African-American homes of which are 65 to 70 percent single-parent. Of that alarming number, 96 percent of those homes are fatherless. First-born son, do you understand what a position of godly privilege you have to correct this situation? Do you understand how powerful you are in your ability to directly address this crisis in our community? Your acceptance of the role and godly endowment bestowed upon you puts you in the position to speak into the lives of those that surround you and are counting on you. This godly endowment also means that you have your house in order and have risen to the level of a man above reproach. Your selfless and sacrificial role renders you readily available to intercede prayerfully for those seeking your advice. The hardships sons of the African-American community have endured over centuries puts them in some of the greatest positions to handle great obstacles and rise to the occasion as heroes. However, because we lack the understanding and knowledge of Isaiah 55:8-11, the miraculous way in which God prepares us that sometimes seems greatly illogical from the human perspective, we more frequently assume the roles of victims. Oh, how we've bought the lie at such an incredibly high cost!

Here is my challenge and my call to reason to you on this topic: You and I will quickly attest to the fact that an incredibly high percentage of the world's dominant performers and achievers in high pressure and stressful situations come from some of the lowest slums, ghettos, and misfortune our world has to offer. Without statistical research, I will go out on the limb to say 90 percent of categories I am referring to in making my point come from this segment. At one time they were at or below the poverty line. I am speaking of professional athletes, those in basketball, football (NFL or Soccer take your pick), baseball, hockey, and so forth. I am also speaking of the military, the marines, special forces, navy seals, and so forth, just to name a few. These are people that come from or are cut from the same cloth, that of poverty, as you were perhaps. And we quickly offer them world class influential status. Sadly sometimes it is simply out of material success rather than credible virtuous substance. Nevertheless, how rapidly they rise to "hero" status. But I have to admit, they do not accomplish the feat with such grace without incredible resilience achieved by the hand that life dealt them in the slums and ghettos of our world. Why then do you feel that same resilience will not work in your favor; you who don't have the same material wealth?

Allow me to illustrate God's wisdom and how it challenges human logic. I will do so with a story of a very close African-American friend who asked me to stand beside him on his journey to discover where God is taking him. I will call him Lavish because I feel God has lavished him with immense blessings he has yet to uncover, but he is staying and needs to stay the course. The day he truly realizes what God is doing through a retrospective look at his life, I think he will explode with overwhelming emotions and wonderment.

Lavish was raised in one of the toughest ghettos the United States has to offer. He was raised by his mother, and sometime later in life was somewhat accepted into a friend's family who noticed his hardship. Lavish has never been in relationship with his father. Even more incredible, Lavish told me stories of playing in the streets and neighborhood of his childhood with multiple friends who also didn't know their fathers. As kids do the craziest things, he and his buddies would tease each other about not knowing their fathers. However, Lavish was always the coolest of the bunch because he was the only one that could say he knows his father. In essence, Lavish knew who his father was and would frequently take his friends to stand across the street and watch his father's comings and goings from his home. But Lavish never dared to go over to his father and say a word. How cruel it is to know your father and not be able to say a word to him? Or even worse, how can an adult and father not want anything to do with his son as so many years go by?

Regardless of the trauma, Lavish actually turned out to be an incredible young man. My chance to get to know Lavish intimately came after he fell short and got his girlfriend pregnant out of wedlock. As we spoke, he was terribly disappointed because he saw himself beginning to perpetuate the vicious cycle he was dealt by his father. Upon learning the child was going to be a son, he was even more emotionally wrecked. There were some anxieties to address between the mother-to-be and Lavish that caused them to separate and really set a deep fear that he would fail as the father his son needs. It took more than a year of his consistent battle to be the father his son needs for the mother to see his commitment and for her to commit to becoming his wife, which he wanted and pleaded for. She hesitated because there were other children of hers involved that she was not sure he would also accept as his own. This was not an easy choice to make, but they have to walk this journey together by faith that God knows best and truly wants a miraculous union for their family.

In case you missed the "my thoughts are higher than your thoughts" moment in this depiction, *only a sovereign God can prepare a man who knew no father in a unique way to be a father to children that truly need a father as this story has unfolded.* Only God can match up souls from worlds apart who need each other, although sometimes they may not realize how much they need each other.

God gives us unique power when we think we are worthless to make an impact in lives we would never ordinarily think to get involved with. The same African-American families which are 65 to 70 percent single-parent and 96 percent fatherless in this country have all of the resilience and tools necessary to turn the tides on this trend if they will simply see themselves as great miracles waiting to happen rather than victims of the system.

Do you know why we marvel at greatness? Because we usually never expect it or see it coming. Therefore it floors us to be a part of it or watch it. God, however, is never surprised. He has prepared us for greatness; we just have to take the step forward. Are you going to?

Youth of the inner city, slums and ghettos, the fatherless, black, white, Hispanic, Asian, third world countries, it is not your "fault" that you were born where or the way you are. God has supremely setup a great catapult for you to launch onto new heights. You just have to take advantage of that situation now. I know this because He did it for me as well.

Charge to Mothers and Mothers-to-Be

I would be remiss if I didn't make this comment as a cap to this segment. Young women are out there having babies out of wedlock and practically not giving them the best chance at life. The statistics clearly show the figures and progression of this trend. With the help of God, stop that now and quit contributing to the crisis! God had a perfect plan in the creation of Adam and Eve, husband and wife, for the conditional and emotional balance of children. A household in unison under the submission of God the Father is an incredible thing to watch. The fact that the statistics portray such a high rate of failure from single-parent homes is not a novelty. It is a consequence for the blatant disobedience of the culture and society. Women, you have the wherewithal to reject any and every sexual or relational advances from a man that bear no substance of quality as a *man at the city gate*. Use the next chapter to glean a few traits or characteristics you should seek out in a man rather than an offer of empty words that he speaks.

CHAPTER ELEVEN:

Living with Our Choices Moment to Moment

Firstborn son, our society has coached us into living defeated lives. I guarantee you I have proof of my claim. Can you honestly say that when you read the title of this chapter your mind did not begin to reach in to your past for all the wrong and costly decisions (choices) you have made? If you didn't, you are an extremely rare breed. But I am willing to bet that 75 percent of the people reading this book drifted first to the negatives. That, my friend, is a sign of a person who is living or has lived a defeated life.

Instead I want to coach you into living the *victorious life*. I want to coach you into realizing that as men and women of this era, we can also live the victorious lives that we read about in the Bible. Have you personified the words of the apostle James in his book, which describes what true and practical Christian living is? Have you inserted your every being into the Scriptures? Have you read the Pauline letters and personified the confidence with which the apostle speaks and literally visualized yourself powerfully instructing fellow believers and unbelievers? Have you personified the Old Testament stories of Abraham, Joseph, Moses, David and the likes, and visualized yourself being used by God for the protection of His people Israel, as well as the promised Seed? Why haven't you?

Firstborn son, have you resigned to the fact that these men were unbelievably godly and courageous? As such it is impossible to live the kind of productive lives they led. I submit to you that the life of defeat we have bought is a fat lie. We have the opportunity to live a better life with God than most of the above listed men did. Do you realize that the human failures of each of these men included many of the similar acts of sin that we individually commit today and worse? Sins such as lying, murder, adultery, disobedience, rejecting Christ, and more were committed by this group of men collectively although at separate instances. What does your record look like? Have you asked yourself how these men could be so confident and effective in the deliverance of God's Scripture after committing such outrageous acts? More important, most of them didn't have the full written Scripture, the Bible, as we do. Yet we live more defeated. Are you asking yourself how can you be powerful with the execution of God's Scripture in an exemplary manner to your sons and daughters and those you come into contact with?

Firstborn son and friend of mine, do you realize that over 90 percent of the Bible was written to believers. However, our defeated coaching has led us to spend most of our time on the 10 percent written to non-believers, lying to ourselves that this is where God wants the majority of our time. If so, I am sure He would have altered the percentages of the Scripture writings mentioned above to reflect that accordingly. My point is this: 90 percent of the Holy Bible has been written to Christians as an immensely rich resource for victorious living. Yet, Christians live the most defeated lives all wrapped up in sinful indulgence. Christians live defeated, worse than the non-believers, that the latter heap senseless mockery upon the heads of the former without remorse. Due to the defeated living Christians exhibit, we fail to set fear for God in the hearts of sinners. I cheated. I read the book of Revelation, and we win. When was the last time you looked at an athletic event and saw the victorious team looking or being intimidated by the losing team?

Winning new souls for Jesus Christ is extremely important. We are to populate heaven and depopulate hell. The power of victorious Christian living will shake our society to its core greater than an earthquake can. Instead, Christians have dropped the ball on the knowledge and insight of our Lord and fail to understand why we continue to lose precious moral grounds in our societies and communities.

How Do We Live Victorious Lives?

How do we live victorious lives as Christians? How do we live lives that are worthy of the power of the Bible characters mentioned above regardless of the great sins they each committed? I am glad you asked thoughtfully, I was getting worried you wouldn't.

I am speaking with the expectation that you are a Christian who has acknowledged your sins and repented before God in the search of forgiveness. Upon doing that, here is how the apostle Paul described what I have no doubt in my mind, each of these men possessed going forward.

"God can testify how I long for all of you with the affection of Christ Jesus. And this is my prayer: that your love may abound more and more in knowledge and depth of insight, so that you may be able to discern what is best and may be pure and blameless until the day of Christ, filled with the fruit of righteousness that comes through Jesus Christ—to the glory and praise of God" (Phil. 1:8-11).

"For God is my witness how I long for and pursue you all with love, in the tender mercy of Christ Jesus [Himself]! And this I pray: that your love may abound yet more and more and extend to its fullest development in knowledge and all keen insight [that your love may display itself in greater depth of acquaintance and more comprehensive discernment], So that you may surely learn to sense what is vital, and approve and prize what is excellent and of real value [recognizing the highest and the best, and distinguishing the moral differences], and that you may be untainted and pure and unerring and blameless [so that with hearts sincere and certain and unsullied, you may approach] the day of Christ [not stumbling nor causing others to stumble]. May you abound in and be filled with the fruits of righteousness (of right standing with God and right doing) which come through Jesus Christ (the Anointed One), to the honor and praise of God [that His glory may be both manifested and recognized] (Phil. 1:8-11, AMP).

Paul starts off in verse 8 by displaying the example of exactly what he is about to demand in the sense of true victorious living. He said, if I may paraphrase, "My love for you is absolutely based in the person of Jesus Christ and my understanding of Him and His teachings. My love for you is not emotionally or humanly self-driven. If it were based as such, I would be very inconsistent and therefore lose the power and effectiveness with which I address you." Regardless of "what kind" and "all" evil Paul had done in his past as Saul, the moment he chose to make Christ and His teachings the foundation and base of his life, not only was he forgiven with his slate wiped clean so to speak, but he was enveloped by a power he had never known before. This is the power with which he speaks and wishes his readers would also come to understand.

In verse 9 he further exemplifies the proper focus of his love for them by breaking into a precise prayer for them. He prays that their love will flourish and proliferate and extend in a specific direction. He does not just ask for love that is kinder, gentle, or tolerant. He is asking for love that deeply extends in knowledge and insight. He is asking for agape love. That knowledge and insight has to be of something, which we will find in a later verse is Jesus Christ. You see, when Christ interacted with His disciples and followers, He did so in love that bore knowledge and insight. When Christ interacted with the Pharisees and Sadducees, as wells as money-changers in the temple, He did so in love that bore knowledge and insight. Why and how did He do that, and what are the benefits or indicators? Verse 10 tells us.

Verse 10 uses a variety of words to describe the benefits and indicators of love full with knowledge and insight. Those benefits and indicators mentioned are: discernment, purity, blameless, vital, approved, prized, excellent, real value, distinguishing moral differences, untainted, unerring, sincere, certain, unsullied, not stumbling, and not causing others to stumble. All of these terms describe what Christ displayed. Whether it was with His disciples or others, He knew when to hug onto the little children or express love and approval to Mary for spending a year's salary value of perfume for His feet. He knew when to rebuke and love a prostitute (the woman at the well), to eat and drink with sinners, and clear out the temple courts. He knew how to accept and encourage those such as Matthew or Zacchaeus, as despised tax collectors, an oppressive Roman centurion, or Nicodemus, a Pharisee and religious leader who should have known better, and more. Most importantly, because of His knowledge and insight, He knew how to take the abuse and submit to death on the cross for yours and my sins, while we were yet still sinners.

It goes on to say in verse 10 that the ultimate point of the testing of our knowledge and insight is the day of Christ. That specifies that the knowledge and insight has to be of Christ so that we are qualified to victoriously approach the day of Christ.

Firstborn son, verse 11 specifies that this knowledge and insight of Christ is evidenced in productivity by God, through God, and for God. The proliferation ought to be filled with the "fruits of righteousness." It sounds to me like Paul is saying we cannot be so deeply entrenched in the knowledge and keen insight of Jesus Christ without producing fruit. This measure of love just absolutely produces fruit, no questions asked. Because of that right and perfect kind of love, others can't help but notice its manifestation and recognize it.

Firstborn son, Paul does a great job of outlining exactly how each of those flawed men got over the hump. The moment they understood clearly through knowledge and insight who our loving God is, and through the person of Jesus Christ, they achieved the ability to live victorious, powerful, and effective lives for God. God has given you and me very similar opportunities. We have the desire to nurture, love, and live productive lives for those who are deeply dependent on us. We have a calling and passion on our lives to live victorious lives rather then the shameful defeated lives we've been living. More importantly, through the Scripture and our Bible, we have a deeper, cross-referenced, documented knowledge and insight of who our God is than those earlier men had.

Locate the roadmap (Bible teaching), review and navigate it, nurture your sons and daughters with proper love in the knowledgeable and insightfulness of Jesus Christ, and nurture those who depend on you. Remember to put a similar investment in your personal influential sources and the sources of influence you create for your sons and daughters and dependents—those individuals and teachings that consistently produce fruit. The Scripture promises that with those checks and balances in place, it is impossible to be unproductive. It will then be impossible to raise a firstborn son who will not impact his generation and be thrilled to carry on your legacy.

CHAPTER TWELVE:

In Conclusion, What Are the Characteristics of a Firstborn Son?

As I work toward the conclusion of this book it should be clear by now that I am putting a challenge before all parents, especially single parents and fathers, as well as those in position of influence and authority over firstborn sons. You have the remarkable daily responsibility of raising the children and future generation of this country. Your son has to face a greater challenge in his day than any I have described in this book, noting society's blatant disregard for godly family values. You may say, "He is never going to face atrocities and dangers of guerilla warfare in his lifetime."

My response... First of all don't think that the Western Hemisphere, even the great USA, is immune from the deterioration of its streets to utter chaos and lawlessness. Secondly, what is more fearful and harder to deal with? Danger that is obvious and poses a clear and direct threat such as warfare, or danger you never see coming or know where it will come from because of the increasing absence of morality? Far too many of us (Christians included) are absolutely oblivious to the fact that our societies and communities are heading directly into such chaos due to the absence of moral absolutes. I hope this book has opened your eyes to that fact, if they weren't already.

Your son has to be nurtured with the grand desire to impact his generation in an absolutely positive manner. You must pass on your legacy, as well as a wealth of courage and nobility to your firstborn son. It must be a legacy that will continue to propagate many generations after you are long gone from the face of this earth, should the Lord allow time. He must graciously embrace his God-given birthright and pursue it with vigorous conviction; he must absolutely defeat the Esau Disorder.

I don't believe it is fair to leave you without giving you a good look into some components of the legacy that I got from my father and that I plan to pass on to my son and generations to come. I think it is unique that I absolutely began this section with my thoughts completely on what I watched my father display and not on my current life at the moment at all. However, as I completed the list I absolutely saw every component of the life I live now. If you ask anybody who knows me intimately, I am willing to risk that this description fits closely with what you will receive. The thing that is formidably surreal about this is the fact that the matching components are very subliminal indicators for me, hence my shock over how similar we are. These are characteristics that I remember of my father from my childhood and especially during my teenage years.

1) My father was a very stable and dependable character in his community. It didn't matter what walk of life people came from, they had full confidence in Ezechiel Bambolo, Sr. He was simply a teacher at a high school that quickly rose through the ranks to become an administrator. But due to his dependability, he was easily the one who represented the school in various negotiations. He was also the one asked to sit in as acting ambassador of Cameroon to the country of Liberia whenever that diplomatic position was in transition. Yet, every illiterate villager for miles around our campus knew him and accepted him as one easily approachable.

2) My father was a man of God always serving the church. I easily remember his unique start to his prayers as every one that came through those doors would. He was called on to pray so frequently because of his servant attitude. Those famous words were, "Oh, heavenly Father..." He

was a deacon in the church, a Sunday school teacher, the treasurer, and more. But when you met him you would think he was the senior pastor.

3) Noting the previous two characteristics, my father was a non-discriminatory source of discernment and godly wisdom for his fellow man (whether being secular, a different faith, or Christian). I know he loved every opportunity to do that with all his heart. In addition, I think the ones that got the most of his passionate servant's heart in this area were his students. They affectionately called him "Monsieur Bam." Mind you he should have been the most feared or hated man by sometimes unruly teenagers and young adults since he carried the title of Dean of Discipline for a good while.

4) My father was never intimidated or wowed by celebrities, diplomats, or those seeking to harm him. I saw an incredible example of a fully balanced life. He didn't wish to have anything others may have had if he didn't have the same. I never once remember him saying that he wished to be something that he wasn't. I saw him in the midst of a great many diplomatic events. It was great however to see him quite relaxed and confident as someone who knew quite well he was prepared for those circles. Previously in the book, I wrote of his arrest and the attempt to execute him during which I had an opportunity to observe his demeanor. There was another incident in 1980 when a coup d'état occurred in Liberia. Truckloads of soldiers came to our campus to arrest administrators because according to them, the assassinated president had poured government money into the school illegally. My father and the principal of the school were taken into custody. What I remember most was him calmly going out to meet the aggressive soldiers understanding the dangers. He calmly reminded them that this was a school of defenseless students and instructors. He showed how to be anxious for nothing.

5) My father was an avid sports and outdoorsman. He enjoyed boxing, soccer, track and field, and more. He was

a great shooter and rifleman, better than me for sure I'll admit, and a great tracker and hunter. More importantly, he loved to hunt at night alone. We would see him prepare to head out for a hunt by dressing with layers primarily to avoid the malaria bites of mosquitoes. He would take his gun and disappear into the forest on foot for what seemed like days. On most occasions, he killed a deer and would somehow bring that heavy animal all the way home by himself. But there were also fun and character building times. He would wake me up at three or four in the morning to follow him into the forest with a wheelbarrow to bring back a couple of deer. Even more exciting was the skinning and preparing of the meat to be stored in the freezer. We also had some great fishing trips, which I will mention in the next section.

6) My father was a great family man. All of my years growing up in the home, I never saw my father once argue with my mother or scream at her for any reason. I am not saying they never argued. We know they did. It was just that the kids never saw arguments because they were determined to not let us see that. They used the privacy of their room at night for important and critical discussions. He was quite firm and decisive, but he didn't need that kind of a scene of screaming anger to affirm control of his home. He spent a lot of time with his children so we had a strong relationship with him. He began to take me hunting with him and build a relationship at a very early age of about eight to ten years old. Until I was old enough and she became interested in other girl appropriate activities, he would drag my sister along on his hunts. He would also take us boys out on all night catfishing adventures that were a blast of a competition amongst us all. What was most entertaining for those pitch-black African nights was unfortunately getting caught in the nest or paths of aggressive soldier ants. Before you knew what was happening, they would have crawled to places in your clothing you wouldn't wish them to be on your worst enemy. However, the laughter

of watching us all strip practically naked to get them all off was some of the most hilarious and memorable moments of my life. As hard as it was in those days for fathers to find common things to do with their daughters, he also had a great connection there. I also remember him playing tricks on us all at the dinner table as we ate as a family. He would jovially coerce us to play a prank on an unsuspecting child and secretly pass a drink or something of theirs to him several seats away without them knowing. It just brought so much fun and laughter as a family unit as we were happy to victimize a sibling. We would spend dark nights in the backyard singing together as a family, even during the war. What beautiful memories even now in my adult years.

7) My father was extremely generous with all he had, which wasn't much as a person on a teacher's salary. My parents were merely teachers with a low income for what it is worth, yet no greater task has society known than an educator. However, he gave away most of what he earned because people less fortunate would come to him and petition for him to support their children educationally. At any given time through almost thirty years of teaching, my father would have as many as twelve kids on his personal scholarship offering. He was just as generous with his time to help others in need. My parents lost everything they ever worked for in thirty years during the Liberian civil war. But I have no doubt that my siblings and I are fortunate to live the life we do, coming out of pretty significant poverty, because of my parents' generosity. It is through that generosity that I also faithfully believe God has blessed our family, even through the many incidents during the war.

Now if you got nothing out of all of those characteristics that my father passed on down to me, get this: The reason that all of these characteristics were so easily transferred to me is because my father had a deliberate design to do so. You see, he took me everywhere he could so that I observed and learned. It didn't matter whether it was a political event, social gathering, hunting adventure, dispute arbitration and resolution, Baptist convention board session, and so on, I was right by his side to watch and learn. It became innate for me because I was there, and it was subliminally being drilled into me. I love to serve others and invest in people. I respect people for as long as they keep and do not abuse my trust, but absolutely nobody outside of my God leaves me awestruck.

You don't have to attend elaborate events to teach your son solid demeanor. I live in a different world and do so many things that my father didn't do, but the traits that he handed me are easily transferrable. So take your son along (as much as possible) to what you do as long as it is upstanding and righteous. Be a part of his life, and it will all come together for him even if he is on a much grander stage than you when his time comes. The apostle Paul took the same approach with Timothy whom he called his "son in the faith." If you study on Timothy in the Bible you will see how often Paul took Timothy along where he went in a desire to teach. Eventually Paul reached a place of utmost confidence to state that he could send Timothy to accomplish a task knowing he would get it done exactly as Paul would do. That was my dad's intent, and it certainly should be yours if you desire to raise a firstborn son that carries on your legacy of greatness.

In addition, here are some "must have" traits and their definitions to help you begin to structure a birthright for your firstborn son. These are key traits that the legacy you pass on absolutely needs to have:[23]

Passion—a) a strong liking or desire for or devotion to some activity, object, or concept b) Suffering; emphatically, the last suffering of the Savior.

Patience—a) the act of bearing pains or trials calmly or without complaint b) steadfast despite opposition, difficulty, or adversity.

Resolute (decisiveness)—a) marked by firm determination b) the act of making a final choice or judgment about something; to select a course of action

Sacrifice—a) to destroy, surrender or suffer to be lost for the sake of obtaining something b) something given up or lost

Integrity—a) firm adherence to a code of especially moral or artistic values b) the quality or state of being complete or undivided

Responsibility—a) liable to be called on to answer b) liable to be called to account as the primary cause, motive, or agent

Leadership—a) the act or an instance of a person who has commanding authority or influence b) one who goes first

Resilience—a) an ability to recover from or adjust easily to misfortune or change

Wisdom—a) ability to discern inner qualities and relationships; a wise attitude, belief, or course of action b) wisdom is the exercise of sound judgment either in avoiding evils or attempting good

Accountability—a) an obligation or willingness to accept responsibility or to accounts for one's actions. (I'd like to interject the saying here that "everyone needs a Paul, a Barnabas, and a Timothy." A "Paul" is someone that mentors you; a "Barnabas" is a peer, encourager, and someone of equal stature; and a "Timothy" is someone you mentor. Unless you are giving away and teaching what you are receiving, you will get bogged down with too much or have no room to take more.)

Spiritual Awareness—a) having or showing realization, perception, or knowledge of God. ("And we pray this in order that you may live a life worthy of the Lord, and please him in every way: bearing fruit in every good work, growing in the knowledge of God" Col. 1:10)

Teach and demand these traits of your son. Remember he is a child, and he most likely does not know what's best for his future. He is going to resist possibly to the extent of expressing severe hatred for you. I did the same even though I dared not voice those thoughts to my parents. But it is the retrospective look at my life and what God was designing me for all along that reminds me He is in control. God knew every bit of development I needed and designed a masterful tapestry with chaos and confusion on the underside but confidence and beauty in the finished product. Following this process of development may leave you exhausted and confused at times, but that is why the process is inseparable from Jesus Christ. *When we are weak, He is strong.* If we adhere to the Scriptures, we know that God does not lie or make errors. Therefore we stay true to His promises and sanctification of the role of firstborn son.

My Continuing Progress as a Firstborn Son

Today finds me with my family continuing to embrace this journey of a lifetime as the firstborn son. You have heard, in the words of this book, of the lives and events that several of us endured. I want to leave you with some updates and evidences that our Lord continues to pursue a righteous relationship with whomever He has set apart as His own to a special calling. I have an incredibly honorable call to duty on my life. I continue to watch Him do His work in and through me for His goodwill.

The country of Liberia went through a horrible fourteen-year civil war and has finally found a measure of peace. The international community of the United Nations deployed more than fifteen thousand-strong peace keeping force to the country to bring peace. The leader of the rebel force is being tried on criminal charges at the world court in The Hague. The nation broke open a new era in African history by electing the first female president the continent has seen. I returned for the first time after seventeen years in November of 2008 to see a people tired of violence and struggling to rebuild a country that seemed to have been set back some fifty or more years. I returned with a group of newfound friends that have been in post-war Liberia for several years now building and restoring orphanages, an unfortunate result of war. I had a chance to see and reconnect with my adopted siblings whom I had not seen in all those years and barely spoke to prior to my arrival.

My family is doing great as well. All of my immediate siblings are doing great as successful and important components along with their spouses for the good of their families. We are all married, and each has several children of our own. The legacy my father and mother passed down is effectively at work in every family unit, and each of us is deliberately working for the success of the next generation. My parents are the matriarch and patriarch responsible for orchestrating this blessing we have received. It was because of their submission to God that they observe and frequently express how fulfilling it is to see what their children have become.

My wife and I are almost ten years into a very successful marriage restoration, and we have been incredibly blessed as a result. With the addition of children, we are joyously making our adjustments to the Bambolo legacy that will be passed on. The adjustments are primarily determined by the era and community in which we find ourselves. We do not live in the parenting era my parents did and neither will our children live in ours. As such, we have to observe negative concerns and positive promises that family trends indicate of the future and train our children to navigate them well. One key ingredient of the legacy handed down by my parents is their everyday commitment and service to the Word of God and the church. I have firmly embraced that reality for my family. However, the era in which I live has demanded that I take it one step further beyond the denominational family traditions. It demands a deliberate, daily, and active study of God's Word so as to clearly distinguish and refute the intelligent subtleties of false doctrine. The dangers we face also come from within the body of Christ, although they are not the true body. Listen to what Paul had to say to the Galatians, and take heed lest you fall or have fallen prey as well.

> "I am astonished that you are so quickly deserting the one who called you by the grace of Christ and are turning to a different gospel—which is really no gospel at all. Evidently some people are throwing you into confusion and are trying to pervert the gospel of Christ. But even if we or an angel from heaven should preach a gospel other than the one we preached to you, let him be eternally condemned! As we have already said, so now I say again: If anybody is preaching to you a gospel other than what you accepted, let him be eternally condemned! Am I

now trying to win the *approval of men, or of God?* Or am I trying to please men? If I were still trying to please men, I would not be a servant of Christ" (Gal. 1:6-10, italics mine).

What the apostle Paul is speaking of here is that we have allowed traditions (the law) of our churches to override the fact that we heard the Word of God and are saved through faith. Why then do we foolishly fight so hard to be approved by the traditions (such as the bylaws of our churches) of man rather than the substance and evidence of the Scriptures?

"Consider Abraham: 'He believed God, and it was credited to him as righteousness.' Understand, then, that those who believe are children of Abraham. The Scripture foresaw that God would justify the Gentiles by faith, and announced the gospel in advance to Abraham: 'All nations will be blessed through you.' So those who have faith are blessed along with Abraham, the man of faith" (Gal. 3:6-9).

Are you reading, studying, and testing the Word of God to see how true it is and thereby living by faith, or are you living simply what is preached from the pulpit? As much as I like to say this is simply my era, the apostle Paul wrote about it. So, it is clearly not just about the era in which I am a parent. What is true about my era is that we have become incredibly lazier Christians than those of Paul's day. Isn't the Bible God-breathed (alive, well, and relevant) for all time or what?

The days of sending our children off to Sunday school, youth groups or camps, and other religious activities without demonstrating our absolute confidence in the inerrant Scriptures by the life we lead are long gone. The days of approaching Christianity as, "That is just what my family did" is also long gone. That approach is strictly tradition, not Christianity. Our world is rapidly changing, and we must systematically train our children to navigate the Bible. In so doing, we cannot just sit back and trust our favorite youth pastor to do a phenomenal job. We have to be directly involved in the biblical nurturing of our children by removing the double standards in our homes. We have to live righteous lives that preach a living testimony to them every day.

We as parents have to distinguish and shut down the influence of the media and culture that seeks to destroy our faith and gravitate toward those that seek to include the Word of God and the beauty He purposed in His masterful creation. We have to seek out those credible sources in our society that unite God and the culture, have done the relevant studies and observations, and are producing incredible material on how to do so. It is a tough but noble task to know and understand who to accept as credible. I guarantee you there are some wolves in sheep's clothing. First and foremost, test and prove everything against the Word of God and Scriptures of the Holy Bible. Second, there are some great sources available in our society for parents to utilize when faced with tough subject matters. I spend a lot of time using them myself and will give them an "A" grade for the work they do. Here are a few popular ones:

- Family Talk with Dr. James Dobson

- Family Life Today

- Focus on the Family

- New Life Live

I leave you with this truth: My parents had no guarantee that their children, more importantly their firstborn son, would end up in the manner and response to their teaching that is now apparent. As such, there is no magical crystal ball to look into. When it comes to human mannerisms and personality outcomes of our children, there is no experimental data for how we accomplish successful preparation, or we'll have robots. From day one of our children's arrival on this earth, even as identical twins, we begin to tell them apart as individuals mainly due to their manners of response and interaction with others around them and things they come into contact with. You could reach for empirical data on how successful some parents have been, but that is still subjective at best. What I perceive of my son's behavior and personality in an identical event that we have both just observed, may be completely and utterly opposite to your perception. However, what he accomplished by his actions are easily measured by qualitative and quantifiable results achieved. I submit the Bible as our means of measurement.

So, raise your son in the way of the Lord. Let us seek out God's view for why He selected and set apart the role of the first-born son to Himself. I guarantee you it is paramount to our lives, and will render your firstborn son fully prepared for every obstacle he will face, as well as any opportunity of good fortune that allows him to impact his generation. I guarantee you that in more instances than not, his attitude toward obstacles and challenges that come his way will be one of excitement to see how God is going to use him as an instrument of righteousness and greatness.

CHAPTER THIRTEEN:

Transitioning, Launching, and the Blessing

God's timing is always incredibly perfect. Just as I completed this book, the Lord gave me an incredible view into the measure of His grace and a lesson I could not have dreamed of planning. This was absolute assurance for me that my Lord's hand was in the writing of this book. This was assurance that He desires to teach an incredible lesson—one that is completely His and absolutely not mine.

"Grandchildren are the crown of old men, And the glory of sons is their fathers" (Prov. 17:6, NASB).

Children have the responsibility to graciously release their parents to the beauty and splendor of final days of life. Whereas, parents have the responsibility of launching and galvanizing the future of their children by giving them a blessing of approval. That approval practically states that the parents have done their job in training and developing the children, especially the way of Proverbs 22:6. When parents actually take the time to express to adult children how proud they are of the adults they have become, and release and trust them to raise the grandchildren as they see fit, that moment is immaculate. I am tempted to liken that moment to the Father's blessing of the Son at the baptism of Christ, "You are My *Son*, My Beloved! In You I am *well pleased* and find delight!" (See Matthew 3:17.) That statement empowered Christ and launched Him into His ministry and the mission He was sent to accomplish. Parents, trust, release, and launch your children.

Transitioning

As a firstborn son, there are three moments in my life that have been transitions and greatly life-changing for me. Two of those moments I have already described in this book, and I am about to describe what is clearly becoming the third. In a recap, here they are:

1) In 1991, the night before I boarded a plane to come to the USA, my dad informed me that the well-being of the family (especially post war) was now my responsibility.
2) In 1999, my wife and I, barely two years out of college, take on the responsibility of supporting my brothers through college and directing those young lives.
3) In 2010, my parents preparing to return to Africa after an approximately seven-year stay in my home, called a meeting of their sons and their wives to release and launch us with godly parental blessings. In return, we thanked them and ushered them into the last stage of their lives with full appreciation of the excellent preparation they gave us. I am excited to see what this transition brings.

Here is a description of how this third transition unfolded. Parents, especially fathers, you must take advantage of the opportunity of exercising one of life's most powerful ceremonies if the Lord allows. I have spoken to several adult children who crave that moment and vote of confidence from their parents, as opposed to interfering in their adult lives much longer than necessary.

My parents asked for an opportunity to speak to their sons and the respective wives at the same time in one gathering. It would have definitely been all of the children together. But unfortunately, my sister literally lives across the country, and her commitments did not allow her to be present. The beauty of this particular evening's gathering is that the crowns of my parents, their grandchildren, filled the home. There were ten grandchildren between the marriages of three brothers present. The sound of cousins laughing and playing together was a glorious one. No doubt, there were a few cries and complaints from the children as they squabbled over toys and turns at games, but it was a thing of beauty nonetheless since this is what "family" looks like.

My father began the evening by asking for our responses to a letter that he wrote each of his children awhile back. In that letter, he asked us to pursue some family projects and wanted progress reports. There was also a need to gauge candidly the health of each of our marriages. There was also a need to assess the long-term commitment of each of the wives from my mother, one who has been a wife now of over forty-five years. This was her Scripture verse and charge to our wives:

"The wise woman builds her house, but with her own hands the foolish one tears hers down" (Prov. 14:1).

Then came the charge and reiteration of the responsibilities of the firstborn son. It had been almost twenty years since I was first commissioned (if you will allow me to call it that). This time it began with hard evidence they now possessed because of living in my home for several years. They admonished my siblings that they had absolutely no doubt in their minds that I was absolutely committed to the success of everyone in the family. They encouraged them and their wives, as well as my wife, those hard conversations I may request as the firstborn son carried no malicious intent. Instead, they have had the privilege and opportunity to see the deeper intentions of my commitment to the success of the family. Although my brothers and their families reside in different states, there is a need for the grandchildren to be granted regular visits as they were doing that night and grow up through the childhood years developing such long-lasting bonds through play and disagreements. Therefore regular family gatherings of this nature are a necessity.

I was also personally reminded and admonished to maintain a thick skin in times of conflict resolutions. I was asked to expect that hurtful comments may be directed at me in the course of the upcoming years. However, it is my place and duty to maintain my composure in addressing and mitigating family affairs, especially now that several young lives have joined the fold. All of this admonishment was delivered with strong biblical bias at the foundation and well accepted by all, especially me, the firstborn son.

Galvanization and Blessing

There is no doubt of the godly and spiritual pursuit of my parents, but I have always been more aware of how much of a praying woman my mother is. From the day I left home in 1991, it has always been apparent that my mother is an early morning riser and prayer intercessor for her children and family. I have specifically felt her prayers covering me.

It therefore made sense that the emotional and spiritual content and context of this gathering began to rise as they neared the end of their discussion and began to envision their departure and farewell. Although home is on the African continent while all of the children and grandchildren reside in the United States at the moment, my parents deeply feel that God has a job for them to do back home. All of us as a family have had a lot of mixed emotions about their departure. However this is by far greater than comforts and dislikes as God would have it.

As such, by God's design the moment presented itself for the children to release the parents to go in peace. Greater than that however was the act and process of giving our parents full assurance that they had done a terrific job to prepare each of us for marriage, and the rearing of our children. First and foremost this was accomplished by teaching us the Bible and also by the exemplary lives they have lived. As such, we encouraged them to transition into the next phase of life that God has designed for them with peace of mind that we are secure and would do well. No amount of money could buy the blessings of grandchildren and in-laws they have accumulated over the years as a poor African couple. Our families being together now and the health each exhibited was more than enough proof for them to feel confident of success.

In the same token, my parents exhibited their trust in each of the couples and gave us their blessings to go forth and raise our children. They acknowledged doing their best to provide for us with all they could or had and fought to provide for us the best environments to grow and be nurtured regardless of a few bumps along the way. Nevertheless, they were thrilled with the outcome depicted by our lives, as well as the development of their grand-children. All the adults stood in a circle as my mother led us in a prayer of blessings upon us.

I wish I could fully describe all of the emotions and thrills for you in words, but this was an extremely powerful moment of transition for my life as the firstborn son. I cannot describe for you the jolt I felt when it finally dawned on me what was literally taking place before my very eyes. With neither my dad or myself declaring this was the intent of this gathering, God suddenly opened my eyes to see that this was the transitioning, launching, and the blessings being conducted within the Bambolo family. My parents plan to spend several weeks with my sister at her home before their departure for Africa and home. God has been incredibly good to us because I am fully aware that very few fam-ilies get to experience this great moment.

I leave you by saying, in committing these next few years to developing your children, you have to plan for and prepare your family for such a moment as this to solidify the passing on of your legacy, especially to your firstborn son.

APPENDIX A

God's View of the Firstborn Son

"Then say to Pharaoh, 'This is what the LORD says: Israel is my firstborn son, and I told you, "Let my son go, so he may worship me." But you refused to let him go; so I will kill your firstborn son'" (Ex. 4:22-23).

"Consecration of the Firstborn
Then the LORD spoke to Moses, saying, "Sanctify to Me every firstborn, the first offspring of every womb among the sons of Israel, both of man and beast; it belongs to Me" (Ex. 13:1-2, NASB).

"(as it is written in the Law of the Lord, "EVERY firstborn MALE THAT OPENS THE WOMB SHALL BE CALLED HOLY TO THE LORD")" (Luke 2:23, NASB).

"Thus you shall separate the Levites from among the sons of Israel, and the Levites shall be Mine. Then after that the Levites may go in to serve the tent of meeting. But you shall cleanse them and present them as a wave offering; for they are wholly given to Me from among the sons of Israel I have taken them for Myself instead of every first issue of the womb, the firstborn of all the sons of Israel. For every firstborn among the sons of Israel is Mine, among the men and among the animals; on the day that I struck down all the firstborn in the land of Egypt I sanctified them for Myself. But I have taken the Levites instead of every firstborn among the sons of Israel. I have given the Levites as a gift to Aaron and to his sons from among the sons of Israel, to perform the service of the sons of Israel at the tent of meeting and to make atonement on behalf of the sons of Israel, so that there will be no plague among the sons of Israel by their coming near to the sanctuary" (Num. 8:14-19, NASB).

"If a man has two wives, the one loved and the other unloved, and both the loved and the unloved have borne him sons, if the firstborn son belongs to the unloved, then it shall be in the day he wills what he has to his sons, he cannot make the son of the loved the firstborn before the son of the unloved, who is the firstborn. But he shall acknowledge the firstborn, the son of the unloved, by giving him a double portion of all that he has, for he is the beginning of his strength; to him belongs the right of the firstborn" (Deut. 21:15-17, NASB).

"They will come with weeping [in penitence and for joy], pouring out prayers [for the future]. I will lead them back; I will cause them to walk by streams of water and bring them in a straight way in which they will not stumble, for I am a Father to Israel, and Ephraim [Israel] is My firstborn" (Jer. 31:9, AMP).

"Mourning for the One They Pierced

And I will pour out on the house of David and the inhabitants of Jerusalem a spirit of grace and supplication. They will look on me, the one they have pierced, and they will mourn for him as one mourns for an only child, and grieve bitterly for him as one grieves for a firstborn son. On that day the weeping in Jerusalem will be great, like the weeping of Hadad Rimmon in the plain of Megiddo. The land will mourn, each clan by itself, with their wives by themselves: the clan of the house of David and their wives, the clan of the house of Nathan and their wives, the clan of the house of Levi and their wives, the clan of Shimei and their wives, and all the rest of the clans and their wives" (Zech. 12:10-14).

"We are assured and know that [God being a partner in their labor] all things work together and are [fitting into a plan] for good to and for those who love God and are called according to [His] design and purpose. For those whom He foreknew [of whom He was aware and loved beforehand], He also destined from the beginning [foreordaining them] to be molded into the image of His Son [and share inwardly His likeness], that He might become the firstborn among many brethren. And those whom He thus foreordained, He also called; and those whom He called, He also justified (acquitted, made righteous, putting them into right standing with Himself). And those whom He justified, He also glorified [raising them to a heavenly dignity and condition or state of being]" (Rom. 8:28-30, AMP).

APPENDIX B

Essence and Roles Scriptural Verses

Essence of the Trinity

"In the beginning was the Word, and the Word was with God, and the Word was God" (John 1:1).

"So, because Jesus was doing these things on the Sabbath, the Jews persecuted him. Jesus said to them, 'My Father is always at his work to this very day, and I, too, am working.' For this reason the Jews tried all the harder to kill him; not only was he breaking the Sabbath, but he was even calling God his own Father, *making himself equal* with God" (John 5:16-18, italics mine).

Essence of Couples, Man and Woman

"But since there is so much immorality, each man should have his own wife, and each woman her own husband. The husband should fulfill his marital duty to his wife, and likewise the wife to her husband. The wife's body does not belong to her alone but also to her husband. In the same way, the husband's body does not belong to him alone but also to his wife" (1 Cor. 7:2-4).

"You are all sons of God through faith in Christ Jesus, for all of you who were baptized into Christ have clothed yourselves with Christ. There is neither Jew nor Greek, slave nor free, male nor female, for *you are all one* in Christ Jesus" (Gal. 3:26-28, italics mine).

Roles of the Trinity

"yet for us there is but one God, the Father, from whom all things came and for whom we live; and there is but one Lord, Jesus Christ, through whom all things came and through whom we live" (1 Cor. 8:6).

"Jesus replied, 'If anyone loves me, he will obey my teaching. My Father will love him, and we will come to him and make our home with him. He who does not love me will not obey my teaching. These words you hear are not my own; they belong to the Father who *sent* me. All this I have *spoken* while still with you. But the Counselor, the Holy Spirit, whom the Father will send in my name, will *teach* you all things and will remind you of everything I have said to you'" (John 14:23-26, italics mine).

"But when the time had fully come, God sent his Son, born of a woman, born under law, to redeem those under law, that we might receive the full rights of sons. Because you are sons, God sent the Spirit of his Son into our hearts, the Spirit who calls out, 'Abba, Father'" (Gal. 4:4-6).

Roles of Couples, Man and Woman

"Wives, *submit* to your husbands as to the Lord. For the husband is the head of the wife as Christ is the head of the church, his body, of which he is the Savior. Now as the church submits to Christ, so also wives should submit to their husbands in everything. Husbands, *love* your wives, just *as Christ loved* the church and gave himself up for her to make her holy, cleansing her by the washing with water through the word, and to present her to himself as a radiant church, without stain or wrinkle or any other blemish, but holy and blameless. In this same way, husbands ought to love their wives as their own bodies. He who loves his wife loves himself. After all, no one ever hated his own body, but he feeds and cares for it, just as Christ does the church—for we are members of his body. 'For this reason a man will leave his father and mother and be united to his wife, and the two will become one flesh.' This is a profound mystery—but I am talking about Christ and the church. However, each one of you also must love his wife as he loves himself, and the wife must respect her husband" (Eph. 5:22-23, italics mine).

"Wives, in the same way *be submissive* to your husbands so that, if any of them do not believe the word, they may be won over without words by the behavior of their wives, when they see the purity and reverence of your lives. Your beauty should not come from outward adornment, such as braided hair and the wearing of gold jewelry and fine clothes. Instead, it should be that of your inner self, the unfading beauty of a gentle and quiet spirit, which is of great worth in God's sight. For this is the way the holy women of the past who put their hope in God used to make themselves beautiful. They were submissive to their own husbands, like Sarah, who obeyed Abraham and called him her master. You are her daughters if you do what is right and do not give way to fear. Husbands, in the same way *be considerate* as you live with your wives, and treat them with respect as the weaker partner and as heirs with you of the gracious gift of life, so that nothing will hinder your prayers" (1 Pet. 3:1-7, italics mine).

WORKS CITED

1. Website: Single Parent Success Foundation. http://www. singleparentsuccess.org/stats.html (26 January 2011).

2. Website: Childstats.gov, Forum on Child and Family Statistics http://www.childstats.gov/americaschildren09 /famsoc1.asp (26 January 2011). Statistic source: U.S. Census Bureau, , Annual Social and Economic Supplements.

3. Child and Family Statistics http://www.childstats.gov/ americaschildren09/famsoc2.asp (26 January 2011). Statistic source: National Center for Health Statistics, National Vital Statistics System.

4. Child and Family Statistics http://www.childstats.gov/ americaschildren09/eco1.asp (26 January 2011). Statistic source: U.S. Census Bureau, Current Population Survey, Annual Social and Economic Supplements.

5. Child and Family Statistics http://www.childstats.gov/ americaschildren09/beh2.asp (26 January 2011). Statistic source: National Institute on Drug Abuse, Monitoring the Future Survey.

6. Child and Family Statistics http://www.childstats.gov/ americaschildren09/beh4.asp (26 January 2011). Statistic source: Centers for Disease Control and Prevention,

National Center for Chronic Disease Prevention and Health Promotion, Youth Risk Behavior Surveillance System.

7. "curse." *Merriam-Webster Online Dictionary.* 2011. http:// www.merriam-webster.com (26 January 2011).

8. Ibid., "gift."

9. Ibid., "purpose."

10. Ibid., "passion."

11. Website: Antioch Networks International (1996—2010). Bible study tools: *W.E. Vine's M.A., Expository Dictionary of New Testament Words* (1940), "godly." http://www antioch.com.sg/cgi-bin/bible/vines/get_defn.pl?num= 1218#C1 (26 January 2011).

12. "legacy." *Merriam-Webster Online.*

13. "purity." *American Dictionary of the English Language.* (Noah Webster, 1828) http://1828.mshaffer.com/ (26 January 2011).

14. Website: FoxNews.com, "Poll: Support for Health Care Reform Tepid as More Americans Oppose Legislation" (FoxNews.com, September 8, 2009). http://www. foxnews.com/politics/2009/09/08/poll-support-health-care-reform-tepid-americans-oppose-legislation/

15. Website: FoxNews.com, "Poll: Public Disapproval for 'Obamacare' Jumps to 52 Percent," (Associated Press, September 9, 2009). http://www.foxnews.com/politics/2009/09/09/poll-public-disapproval-obamacare-jumps-percent/

16. Website: CNN Politics, Political Ticker, "Poll: Double-digit post-speech jump for Obama plan," (CNN, September 10, 2009). http://politicalticker.blogs.cnn.com/2009/09/10/cnn-poll-double-digit-post-speech-jump-for-obama-plan/

17. Steven Ertelt, "CNN Spins Poll Following Obama Speech Favoring Pro-Abortion Health Care Bill," (LifeNews.com, September 10, 2009). http://www.lifenews.com/2009/09/10/nat-5455/

18. Website: SupremeCourtCases.com, Eastern Book Co. (1998-2011). Dr. Mahendra Tiwari, "Freedom of press in India: Constitutional Perspectives," (December 7, 2006). http://www.supremecourtcases.com/index-prac-ticallawyer.php?option=com_content&task=view&id=6752&Itemid=1

19. Dr. Karl I. Payne, *Transferable Cross Training 2: Apologetics* (Redmond, WA: Transferable Cross Training, 2004), 24—25.

20. "tolerance." *Merriam-Webster Online.*

21. Website: WinWisdom Quotations. Joseph Barber Lightfoot was a preacher from the 1890s. Here you will find several quotations from him including the one in this text: http://www.winwisdom.com/quotes/author/joseph-b-lightfoot.aspx

21. Child and Family Statistics http://www.childstats.gov/americaschildren09/fam-soc1.asp (26 January 2011). Statistic source: U.S. Census Bureau, , Annual Social and Economic Supplements.

23. The foundations for defining these traits are paraphrased from Noah Webster's 1828 dictionary, an invaluable resource. The biblical connotations of the definitions are outstanding. *American Dictionary of the English Language.* (Noah Webster, 1828) http://1828.mshaffer.com/ (26 January 2011).

CPSIA information can be obtained at www.ICGtesting.com
Printed in the USA
LVOW122310150413

329296LV00001B/12/P